Wildflowers on the Windowsill

By Susan Tyler Hitchcock

GATHER YE WILD THINGS: *A Forager's Year*

MONTICELLO AND BEYOND: *Charlottesville, Albemarle County, and The University of Virginia*

A GUIDE TO GROWING
WILD PLANTS INDOORS

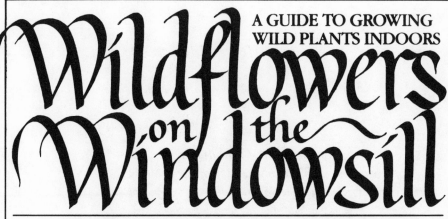

Wildflowers on the Windowsill

SUSAN TYLER HITCHCOCK

ILLUSTRATED BY G. B. McINTOSH

CROWN PUBLISHERS, INC.   NEW YORK

Published by Crown Publishers, Inc.,
One Park Avenue, New York, New York 10016
and simultaneously in Canada by General Publishing Company Limited
Manufactured in the United States of America
Library of Congress Cataloging in Publication Data
Hitchcock, Susan Tyler.
Wildflowers on the windowsill.
1. Wild flower gardening.   2. Indoor gardening.
I. Title.
SB439.H57   1983   635.9'676   83-14320
ISBN 0-517-55190-X
Calligraphy by David Gati
Book design by Camilla Filancia
10 9 8 7 6 5 4 3 2 1
First Edition

CONTENTS

Contents

A C K N O W L E D G M E N T S

I wish that I could have gained from the knowledge and experience of the many expert windowsill gardeners across the continent who have, either by chance or design, grown wildflowers on windowsills before me. As it was, I managed to contact only those few fanatical wildflower lovers I knew, and those few did indeed contribute much to the project.

Thank you to Jerome Wexler, who proposed the initial idea for the project. Thank you to Nahum Waxman, whose early interest kept the idea alive and helped it approach book form. Thank you to Pamela Thomas, who saw it through to publication. Thank you to Naomi Kleinberg and Sheila Gaffney for helping with the details of publication. Thank you to New York taxi cab driver Herbert Grice, without whose goodwill these pages would look very different. Thank you to Ann Joseph for putting these words on paper so neatly and promptly. Thanks to Robert Baur, William Chapman, Kathi Keville, Bill Roody, and Billy Joe Tatum for their expert advice and wise suggestions.

And thanks to David Watkins, my husband, for doing all he could to help me stay serenely at the typewriter.

My thumb's only a dull shade of green. I love the plant world. I live amid nature. Plants play a part in almost everything I do. I take great pleasure in fostering greenery, but I can't say I always succeed.

And yet I'm always surprised at how well wild plants take care of themselves. No one plants them, no one waters them, no one fertilizes them. Still they take over. In the garden, in the lawn, in the greenhouse, even in the soil surrounding potted houseplants, wild plants thrive. If they're so good at growing, I began to ask myself, why don't we pot them instead?

I've spent several years now pursuing answers to this question, trying to discover which wild plants do well in pots indoors, which ones don't, and what one must do to take care of those that don't mind the transition. I discovered that no one had written a book on this subject so far. There are shelves full of books about caring for houseplants, but they all deal with the tropical plants you buy at the store. There is at least one shelf full of books about growing wildflowers, but their concern is with transplanting wild plants into an outdoor garden. No books, so far as my editors and I could discover, have devoted themselves exclusively to bringing wild plants indoors. Hmmmmmm, I thought, wonder why? I've spent a few years wondering.

To answer briefly, it's not that simple to grow wild plants inside.

The weeds you see out there, merrily growing on their own, have found soil, light, moisture, minerals just to their liking. If conditions aren't right, the generations of plants set no seed, the plants die out, and today they wouldn't be growing there. If conditions are right, generations of plants propagate fiercely, creating the mess of weeds I'm looking

at out of my study window right now. They found just the right combination of conditions, but for *me* to discover what they need is quite
another matter.

I suppose that a soil scientist might be able, through geological and
chemical analyses, to give me pertinent details of the growing medium a
wild plant has chosen. Then I would have to turn to a physicist to learn
the intensity and color range of light it chose. Then a meteorologist could
measure rainfall, and whatever other indicators of moisture in the environment I would need to understand what water level the plant needs
in soil and air around it. And then I would have to translate all their data
into practical knowhow: potting soil, fertilizer, window or artificial light,
watering methods and schedules.

The tried-and-true method, learning to grow plants by doing it,
seems instead the best method for me. And that's the method I've followed in writing this book.

But as I say, my thumb's just dull green. I'll be the first to admit I've
seen failures on my windowsill. And I'm more than half the time inclined
to take the burden on myself, to say "I didn't learn to grow that plant
right" rather than to say "That plant died on me."

Within limits. I started this project blithely, with the notion that the
brightest of summer's field flowers, daisies and buttercups, could
blossom on my windowsill too: Queen Anne's lace bending over my
plant stand, black-eyed Susans smiling at me. But I've had to admit my
limits, and I've tried to take into account the limits of most experimental
wild-plant potters too.

Some of my favorite wildflowers just won't grow on my windowsill.
If perhaps someday I should find myself in a home with a walk-in greenhouse, where light levels approximate the brilliance of sunshine outside,
then perhaps I'll take up the challenge of daisies and buttercups. But for
the purpose of this book, I stuck with plants that would grow in limited
space and light—either an east-, south-, or west-facing window or under
a small grow-light fixture.

And for the purpose of this project, I cautiously tried to gather and
test those plants which grow in such abundance that I wouldn't be rob-
bing the wild of their kind if I dug a few to bring inside. Any author of a
book on gathering wild things, whether the gathering is for culinary or

for decorative purposes, must concern herself not just with the effects of her own continued gathering, but with those of her readers whom she hopes to influence and guide. The possibility that by writing a book such as this one I might actually contribute to the disappearance of even one plant species haunts me throughout my work.

Extreme conservationists may not agree with my solution to that problem, which is to find a middle way. I find myself in league with game hunters, oddly enough, who claim that they know better than anyone the value of maintaining the species that they hunt. Analogously, those who gather wild plants do so out of educated interest and respect for the native habitats in which they find them. More than the uninformed idler in the forest, an educated gatherer of wild things knows the importance of maintaining the livelihood of the wild.

I get into deeper water when I use this argument to defend gathering wild plants for decorative purposes, as compared with gathering wild plants to eat. First of all, eating is more essential to survival than appearances, and lessons in gathering food are defensible in view of the dim possibility of a need to survive with no other sustenance. We could get along very nicely during a catastrophe without wildflowers on the windowsill.

Second, one who gathers wild things for food has an urgent need to see the next year's crop survive, or else supplies will be depleted. But the one who gathers a wild plant for windowsill decoration may not be concerned—so the argument might be stated—since with proper care, that potted wild plant could suffice forever, never mind what remains in the wild.

Furthermore, anyone can go out and gather a good-looking plant, bring it home, and try to get it to grow on a windowsill, no risks involved. But go out to gather a good-looking plant to serve to friends and family for dinner? Even the most ignorant know they ought to learn a little before doing that. You don't have to know the name or chemical content of a plant to grow it on the windowsill, let alone know whether it's rare or endangered.

For these quite serious reasons, I have conceived this book in harmony with a strong conviction that the major reason one should even gather wild plants for the windowsill is so that one can learn more about the world of wild plants outside. I encourage the gathering of common, beautiful wild plants, and in the same breath I encourage the study of their native habits and habitats and those of their rarer kindred. Observing the patterns of growth among wild plants leads to an awareness of how human culture may interfere with those patterns. For many people, those patterns can be more closely observed at home, rather than in the wild. But their meaning in the ongoing cycle of nature holds true only when wild plants still thrive in their own homeland. Indeed, we can hinder that cycle; yet we can harmonize with it as well.

It's out of concern for these issues that certain plants won't appear here—spring beauty, jack-in-the-pulpit, columbine—plants I'd love to see springing out in my terrarium, plants I'd love to watch unfold on my windowsill. But they are too precious in our forestland, too precarious in the scheme of things, to warrant risking failure as I try to bring them home. By and large, the plants listed in this book grow abundantly enough that I do not hesitate to experiment. Many of them are pulled up and cast out as weeds. Others may be borderline cases, like the club mosses and maidenhair fern. Every wild plant gatherer must take the responsibility to determine the prevalence of plants she wishes to gather in her own locale. I have tried to suggest ways of gathering that won't deplete the wild. It's a tricky business, treading the line between conservation and curiosity. I hope my effort doesn't come off sounding too ambiguous at times.

The search goes on. Despite my thumb of dull green, I'll keep on trying. I've got a speedwell and an everlasting growing on my windowsill that didn't find their way into this book, simply because I just gathered them yesterday. I hope that my message, to those of you still in tune with its design, inspires inquiring enthusiasm more than a dogged effort to follow my rules. Chances are your backyard's full of adoptable wild plants, maybe different from those that grow in my own. Chances are your thumb's a bit more green than mine is. Chances are you'll find your own world of windowsill wildflowers, and I hope it's with sunshine and success that you do.

Wildflowers on the Windowsill

CHAPTER 1

Bringing Wild Plants Indoors

It seems so simple and obvious, gathering houseplants from the wild. And yet of all the thriving sprays of greenery perched on windowsills today, I'd venture that fewer than 1 percent of them are native to the neighborhood. We've been conditioned to consider tropical imports appropriate for indoor growing, while native wild plants belong outside. We've been conditioned, I might add, to *buy* plants to grow indoors, while in the very same afternoon that one went shopping for new houseplants one may have spent an hour weeding the garden, pulling up and chucking out other healthy plants, equally beautiful in their own wild way.

And why?

History offers good reasons. The very idea of growing plants inside gained popularity during the mid-nineteenth century. Botanical foragers brought plants back from South America that could withstand the rigors of indoor life. In their own environment, those plants formed the middle strata of native rain forests. They dwelt below the dense leafy canopy of the tallest trees, where light was diffuse and dim. Although they benefited from steamy humidity, they endured dry spells as well. Little light, sporadic watering, extremes requiring adaptation—newfound tropical plants weathered these conditions in the tropics, and the same conditions awaited a houseplant brought into a Victorian home. Tropical plants seemed ready to face the challenge. Most wild plants weren't.

An exotic mystique surrounded those tropical plants as well, and perhaps for some people it still does today: palm trees in the conservatory, papyrus in the parlor. But today many people (including myself) get to feeling ho-hum about the ever-present houseplants on the market: philodendron, pothos, shefflera, dracaena. You look around at the wilder corners of the out-of-doors—in your yard, at vacation scenery in parks and forests—and you notice the beautiful shapes of plant life growing all around you, nowadays as exotic as tropical imports were back then.

Almost every wild plant growing in a temperate climate will require different care than will the tropical plants you've already grown at home. As much as it might be chalked up as a fluke of horticultural history, there are good reasons why tropical plants were the first to come indoors. Wild plants generally need more light, more constant watering, and more nourishment than the plants we're used to growing in our homes. And to top it all off, some wild plants will die back in winter, even if they're grown inside. You won't find a tropical houseplant doing that to you.

But for those who enjoy the challenge of learning to grow a plant indoors that has not already proved successful for millions, for those who share a love of the natural world that thrives around them, for those who like the idea of opening up a whole new world of plants to get to know, growing wildflowers on the windowsill can be a satisfying pastime. It's an irony at the heart of the houseplant industry, to think that a common weed makes a more exotic houseplant than some faraway jungle's vine.

Our homes are now better prepared to grow any kind of houseplant than were homes a century ago. We design with more glass, including picture windows, skylights, even attached greenhouse space. We have learned the mechanics of heat conservation, heat distribution, and insulation, so that our houses don't go through extreme temperature dips in winter. We have machinery and construction techniques for cooling and venting, so summer heat doesn't bake us or our houseplants. Homes are less often heated by wood burned indoors, and even when they are, modern householders know enough to counteract the hot, dry air with some method of humidification. Indoor houseplants appreciate these manifestations of progress.

They also appreciate advances in the technology of artificial lighting. As plant scientists have learned more about plants' light needs, electrical engineers have met those needs with new light-bulb designs. In the last quarter century the role of the various colors or wavelengths of light, all of which combine in the white light of sunlight, has been studied and applied in the invention of numerous commercial grow-lights. With electricity wired into our homes and now with these bulbs, designed to meet plant needs more closely than ever, many of the plants overlooked years back as houseplants can be reconsidered, among them some native wildflowers.

But not all wildflowers, I hasten to add. I've tried growing a lot of wild plants now, under grow-lights as well as in the window. I quickly had to alter the outline of this book, once I discovered that I was facing inevitable defeat every time I tried to grow a summer field flower indoors, even under lights. Grow-lights may replicate the diffuse light of spring or autumn. There are a few undemanding summer blooms they might bring on. But wild plants that carry a showy summer bloom on a slender stalk—Queen Anne's lace, black-eyed Susans, daisies, buttercups, and the like—won't bloom on a windowsill or in a grow-light environment. Perhaps potted on an exposed porch or in a greenhouse that offered close to the full array of summer sunlight, they would bloom. But to keep my experiments within the realm of possibility for most readers, I limited my own experiment stations to windowsills and a relatively low-intensity grow-light. That decision limited my results.

Certain constant rules of thumb should guide the gathering and growing of wild plants. I outline those rules. But each plant has its own needs, its own habits. Sensitivity to these particulars makes for a more successful windowsill wild garden. Besides the beauty and the thrill of perpetuating life, developing a sensitivity to wild plants and their customs becomes the greatest reward in growing wildflowers on the windowsill. Take a walk in the woods and you learn much about native wildflowers. Bring one of those wildflowers home with you—germinate a seed, start a cutting, see a rootlet sprout—and you come to marvel even more at the diversity and balance of forces alive in the natural world, independent of any effort of the human mind or hands.

At first glance, the daily life of plants seems unchanging. Plants don't move unless a wind breezes by. Plants don't seem to sleep or wake. But in the larger picture, we know that plants revolve with the day, just as animals do.

Occasionally a plant's daily cycle shows through clearly, as in some species of oxalis that fold up their leaves at evening. This outwardly visible movement reflects changes within the plant's system. The phase of photosynthesis that captures light and converts it to food energy occurs only when the sun is shining. (A correspondent "dark" phase of photosynthesis, which bundles that energy for storage, can proceed in the dark.) The sun has other effects on a plant as well, including the forceful suction of evaporation, drawing moisture out of the leaves. Plants act as conduits in the cycles of water moving between earth and sky, and so they respond daily, hourly, to changes in the atmosphere. Watch those oxalis plants fold up on a rainy day or on a day so blistering that to keep conduction channels open would mean dehydration and death to the plant.

Those who gather wild plants must respect these daily cycles, especially during summertime. When you uproot a plant, you are temporarily intercepting the lower end of that water-conduction channel. If you do so at a time when the upper end—the pores or "stomata" in the leaves—are wide open, as they are in response to the bright light of midday, you risk a total wilt that may prove hard to revive. With no more water coming in through the roots and water still pouring out through the leaves, the plant becomes desiccated, its cells collapse, and it wilts.

To avoid this disaster, gather living plants at a time of day or during weather in which the plant is less vulnerable: early morning, late afternoon, or evening, or during an overcast or rainy day. During the spring autumn, and winter months, these rules matter less, as also in the case of gathering shade-dwelling plants. But in general, remember that the toughest period through which you'll put that plant is the first week of transplantation. Might as well pamper it as much as you can.

Annual cycles should guide you in your gathering just as much as daily cycles should. Some of the plants included in this book thrive in the desert or West Coast zones where seasons do not change with great intensity. But others grow in zones with four distinct seasons, and their growing patterns reflect that environment, each one differently.

Spring is usually the time for establishment, whether it's a perennial sprouting green anew, a biennial emerging from last year's beginnings, or an annual sprouting from seed. Spring can also be a time for flowering, and the wild plant gatherer should respect the fact that green growth often defers to the development of a flower when the time is right. Summer represents the time of lushest growth for most plants, although not for all of them. Autumn is often storage time, whether that means setting seed or sending sugars down into underground rootstock to last through winter till spring sprouts again.

Just as someone foraging for edible wild things must know the seasons for the hunt, so the same understanding of each plant's annual cycle must govern gathering wild plants for the windowsill. Some are best gathered in spring, when they're small and manageable and show promise of growth. Some may not appear until summer. Some plants will respond to autumn breezes by dying back, even on your windowsill. Knowing that, you may still choose to gather them in autumn to enjoy a spring sprouting, or you may instead pass those plants by for the ones that rise to dominance in autumn and winter, since they'll soon thrive on your windowsill.

For those who wish to gather seeds and cuttings from wild plants— an excellent way to bring green life home without tampering with the wild—annual growing cycles matter, too. Seed heads from some plants ripen and shatter quickly, so gathering them at the right time is crucial to success. Healthy cuttings from leafstalks are best gathered at the plant's peak of growth—in most cases, mid- to late summer. Healthy cuttings from root systems are best gathered at the plant's ebb of growth—in late autumn or winter, when the year's growth has been stored underground.

Sprouting seed requires more patience and control than transplanting from the wild. Not only the gathering and separating of seed from stalk but also the process of germination require diligence. Many of the most common weeds, which are the plants I've used for sprouting, seem not to require "vernalization": the creation of a little winter for the seed. If you venture beyond examples in this book in your efforts to sprout wild seed, remember that if you live in a climate where winter freezes over, the plant seeds you gather may need that freeze to sprout. Wrap them in a dry paper towel and a plastic bag and leave them in the freezer for about six weeks. Botanical records about the needs of wild plant seeds are hard to find, so you may have to conduct a few experiments on your own.

Making a Home for Wild Plants

Many of the practices you're already following, if you're successful at growing houseplants, will serve you well in the day-to-day care of growing wild plants. Just a few refinements, a few adjustments to respond to wild plants' needs, will enlarge your repertoire of plants grown at home significantly.

Choosing the pot in which to put a plant involves considerations both practical and aesthetic. Clay pots have a natural, earthy appearance. They are porous, allowing moisture and air to flow in and out of the sides of the pot. But that same quality also means that they retain less moisture over time than their plastic counterparts. Many wild plants require more frequent watering than common houseplants, chosen for their minimal needs. So despite the odd juxtaposition—going natural with wild plants and going synthetic with plastic pots—I've inclined toward plastic. Some wild plants, nevertheless, are suitable for clay pots, though they may need watering more often. Yucca is a good example. At the other extreme, some wild plants (bedstraw, for example) need such moist soil to support them that a clay-pot environment would require more than daily watering. I've made that mistake enough times that I've learned to avoid it.

What about decorator pots—glazed ceramic, Lucite, glass? Each of these materials shares with plain old plastic a high rate of moisture retention, so that they should serve you very well. Watch out for pots with no drainage holes at the bottom, however, and use those only for plants like yucca or aloe whose native environments reveal that they can do without regular watering. The problem with drainless pots is that excess watering causes rotting from down under, and often it will destroy a plant before you know what's the matter. If you pot a slow-growing plant with low moisture needs in a pot without holes in the bottom, be sure to water it infrequently and it should do fine.

Of course, it's not just the pot that determines the moisture-holding qualities of your windowsill garden. The composition of the soil in your pots will make a big difference too. The wild plants featured in this book grow naturally in a variety of soil types, from the humus-rich leaf mold of an eastern forest soil to the dry, sandy soil of the desert. Try to replicate the soil environment in which you found your wild plant growing, and you've taken a first important step in creating a proper world for the wild plant in your home.

Since many of the plants in this book represent common roadside or pasture weeds, I have come up with a basic recipe for wild plant potting soil that remains constant throughout. Here and there I will suggest variations on the recipe, to respond to particular needs of a plant. But the wild plant potting soil, a variation on the houseplant potting soil mix often prescribed in other books, will serve for the majority of plants listed here, and many others. You may wish simply to mix a large quantity of the stuff, then cover it and keep it on hand for whenever you want to sprout or transplant something new.

Wild Plant Potting Soil

3 parts potting soil, sifted garden soil, or sifted compost
1 part perlite, sand, or fine gravel
1 part vermiculite or humus

Let's look into each of the components, one by one.

Store-bought potting soil (not a mix all ready) is made primarily from peat moss, humus, or other organic material mass-collected from major deposits around the world, sifted and sterilized for you. It is fine, regular in consistency, and dependable in its cleanliness and healthfulness for plants. It also costs a bundle. Those who live in a situation where soil is plentiful—gardeners, or those with access to rich forest soil—may cringe at the idea of buying soil, and may wish instead to use the soil available to them. Enriched garden soil or—richest of all—garden compost may be substituted in the recipe for store-bought soil, but risks arise with that substitution. Sifting will take care of worms, bugs, stones, twigs, and other miscellaneous items that creep and hide in soil outside. But sifting won't take care of microscopic creatures, some bad and some good, dwelling in the soil. I must admit a personal inclination *not* to sterilize garden or forest soil, but many experts in the field would disagree, believing that harmful microscopic elements outnumber the beneficial. For the record, I will offer instructions on how to sterilize soil, and leave it up to each reader to decide.

Spread sifted soil in a baking pan with sides one to two inches tall. Cover with a lid or a sheet of aluminum foil, then place in a 300-degree oven for an hour. Let the soil cool before mixing with other ingredients in the wild plant potting soil mixture.

The natural inclination, when gathering plants from the wild, is to want to bring home wild soil in which to grow them, the very soil in which they grew in their native home. The inclination can be followed if one also adheres to certain rules. When uprooting a wild plant, leave the roots embedded in a ball of soil for the journey home. But once home, gently persuade the roots out by breaking up the soil around them. Speedily set them into a pot where the soil is loose and friable, thus providing the best environment for root regeneration and growth. Roots bound within a soil ball, even if it is the soil the plant chose on its own, often never penetrate into the new soil environment, and their growth is severely limited. Furthermore, in a densely packed soil ball surrounding a wild plant's roots all kinds of other creatures may be dwelling. In the wild, they might not harm the plant, but potted up they can wreak havoc. All the more reason to remove wild soil from the roots of a plant you've gathered. Sift it, sterilize it if you like, then replenish the pot with that wild soil, rather than just plunking plant and all into a pot.

The other constituents of our wild plant potting soil enrich its growing capacity in two different ways. Perlite, sand, or fine gravel serves to aerate the soil. Because these little granules are impermeable and have jagged edges, they actually create pockets through which water can seep and air can circulate. They keep the potting soil from packing down. Vermiculite and humus absorb and hold more water than the soil itself, and by adding them to the potting soil we increase its overall ability to retain the moisture needed in such high quantities by many wild plants. For ferns, the potting soil recipe requires even higher amounts of humus. For aloe, it needs less humus, but more perlite or sand. Specific variations on the potting soil recipe will be mentioned according to each wild plant's needs.

Water and light are the raw materials from which every plant makes its own food, so watering and lighting practices are crucial to growing any plant indoors successfully. Here is the very best rule of thumb for when to water a houseplant, wild or tame: When the soil feels dry to the touch, water throroughly enough so that the water seeps out the pot's drainage holes below. If you have created a porous soil according to the recipe and if you have set the plant in well enough that its roots spread out through the soil, water seeping out the bottom assures you that water is permeating the pot as well. Don't let the pot stand in water—empty the saucer beneath promptly—but do use this method to double-check the thoroughness with which you water.

Lighting can be a major factor in the success or failure of any indoor plant, wild plants particularly. The comparative intensities of light indoors and outside can be elusive, but anyone who has used a light meter to adjust camera settings, even between a cloudy day and a brightly lit room, knows how much more brightly the sun shines than does our indoor lighting. Windows seem to let light stream in, but they can't offer the 360-degree exposure of outdoor plant sites. Even in a south-facing window, and certainly in those facing east or west, the hours of daylight available to a plant are limited. As the summer sun climbs higher overhead around the solstice, roofs and windowframes limit its reach inside even further.

What these comparisons mean to the windowsill wild plant gardener is that indoor lighting levels greatly limit the numbers and types of wild plants that can be grown indoors. Even a summer wildflower that can manage to bloom in forest shadows gets more light—higher intensity, longer daylight hours—then any indoor window exposure can give. Exceptions to this rule may include sunrooms, where windows bring in light from two or three directions and for many hours of the day. Other exceptions may include porches or balconies for the very same reason, but often their building structure casts shadows, limiting light almost as much as interior roofs and walls do.

These limitations call for two responses from the enthusiastic grower of wild plants indoors. First, one's choice of which plants to adopt for potting must be governed by one's lighting facilities inside. And second, if one wants to make the effort, one can fabricate growing situations with higher light intensities than one's windows provide. Grow-lights come these days in a variety of shapes and prices, and they do offer indoor gardeners more possibilities without having to depend upon sunlight from outside.

Two principal types of grow-lights are commercially available these days: the incandescent or spotlight type and the fluorescent or tube type. Fluorescent grow-lights come in rings as well, producing a circular halo of light. But most people find tube fixtures easier to incorporate into their homes, and I will limit my comments to them.

Each type of grow-light has its advantages for the plants growing under it. The features it offers must be explained in terms of the light needs of any growing plant. Sunlight, to the eye appearing white, in fact combines all the colors of the rainbow, as the colors cast by a prism vividly display. Physicists describe those components not only in terms of their colors but also in terms of varying lengths in the waves of light. Red light travels in a wavelength of 700 nanometers, blue light in a wavelength of 470 nanometers. (A nanometer equals one ten-millionth of a centimeter.) Plants have special needs for these two wavelengths of light in particular, a fact that can be reasoned from their chlorophyll-green color. That color indicates which wavelength of light the plant cells reflect back out again; the other wavelengths, and primarily red and blue light, are absorbed by plant cells and put to use in photosynthesis.

These details underlie the reasons why we need special grow-lights rather than merely household bulbs. Although its light looks white to the naked eye, the common light bulb casts light in which reds predominate. It's very short on blue. When botanists discovered the importance of blue and red light waves to the growing patterns of green plants, engineers soon began to apply that knowledge to make bulbs different from household bulbs, bulbs that offered blue light as well as red within their rays. That characteristic is the central distinction that makes a grow-light bulb different from an ordinary light bulb.

But grow-light bulbs differ one from another, too. The incandescent or spotlight type, although incorporating blue lightwaves, predominates in red. Incandescent grow-lights, shedding light from a focused center, generate more heat than fluorescent tubes and could burn tender plants if left too close to them. Incandescent bulbs have a shorter life, but fluorescent bulbs diminish in power through extended use too, especially through continually being turned on and off again. Each grow-light has its own strengths and weaknesses, for which reason many indoor horticulturists recommend a grow-light setup that incorporates both.

In my effort to grow wild plants indoors, I constructed such a setup. To my mind, it represented the simplest and least expensive rig with which I could generate plant growth beyond the limits of light coming from outside. I put two 24-inch, 25-watt fluorescent tubes in a standard side-by-side fluorescent fixture. Alongside the tubes, in a movable lamp that could swivel and turn and focus light at appropriate distances on one plant or many, I placed a 150-watt incandescent reflector (or wide-range) bulb. The hours of light I provided my plants averaged about sixteen, from seven in the morning, when I woke up, to eleven at night, when I went to bed. If I went away for an overnight or a weekend, I left the grow-lights burning all the time.

My grow-light rig did not even begin to approximate levels of sunlight in the out-of-doors. Such a setup would not provide adequate lighting for many summer field flowers, for example, accustomed as they are to levels of light reaching at least a hundred times what these few grow-light bulbs can shed. Subsequent experiments in my house or yours may include more complex combinations of incandescent and fluorescent grow-light lamps, brought together to approximate more closely the range and brilliance of sunlight outside. But for the purposes of this book and its initial list of wild plants suitable to bring indoors to grow, I chose to limit my own artificial lighting to a minimum.

Numerous books and articles explain more fully than I can here how to shop for grow-lights, how to attach them to cupboards and walls, how to arrange them and the plants beneath them. Just remember that many wild plants, and particularly those that grow in the full light of a summer's day, depend upon more light than we may ever be able to muster with indoor bulbs. A daisy blooming in an open field on the summer solstice basks in 8,000 foot-candles of light. My grow-light rig provides only about 1,000 foot-candles to the plants set inches from the fluorescent tubes. To boost it to the levels enjoyed by that daisy, I would have to add eighteen tubes and five incandescent grow-light bulbs. I'd have to move out of that room altogether, too. I'd rather leave the daisy outside and bring in plants that put fewer demands on me and my grow-lights.

While water and light form the basic ingredients of green plants' diets, they need other nutrients as well, just as humans do, to ensure a healthy growth rate. We colloquially consider fertilizer "plant food," but it's no more food than the vitamins we take. It provides the trace minerals that keep plant metabolism running right. Wild plants get their fertilizer from natural sources, so if we're going to adopt them, we're going to have to fertilize them, too.

Commercial houseplant fertilizers are blended to encourage green leafy growth, because that's the primary reason most people grow plants indoors. Many wild plants, different from tropical houseplants, vary in their growth rate through the year. Their fertilizer needs vary simultaneously: the more vigorous the growth, the more fertilizer needed. But for those few plants in this book that will bloom indoors, fertilizer may very well discourage the bloom you're trying to coax, since the plant is being prodded toward making more leaves.

For those plants grown for foliage, the following fertilizing schedule should work: once every two months from October to April, once a month the rest of the year. If you're using a commercial fertilizer, mix as indicated for houseplants and fertilize following this schedule. Organic gardeners might prefer to substitute their own manure tea, but they should follow the same schedule as well. Those who hope to force a bloom should double the frequency of fertilizing up to six weeks before expected blooming, then withhold all fertilizer until after the bloom. I watched with dismay as a spiderwort plant, which had been blooming daily for a week, sent out a new leafy shoot days after I absentmindedly watered it with fertilizer I had prepared for other green plants. That marked the end of its flowering for that year, a vivid lesson in why one should withhold fertilizer when plants are in bloom.

Other than these particulars about indoor care for wild plants you've adopted, you can follow the customs of houseplant care that have succeeded for you already. Talk to them, sing to them, move them from window to window, whatever you like to do with your plants to make them feel more at home. Wild plants really aren't all that different from the plants sold for houseplants nowadays. Philodendrons are wild plants somewhere in the world, and dandelions really do take well to potting.

Where and What Not to Gather

The suggestions in this book may make some people shudder out of concern for the future of the wild. Some places are inappropriate locations for the gathering of plants or their parts. Some plants ought never to be gathered. Certain general rules apply throughout the United States, and in addition each state or locality has its own rules, available from wildlife commissions or garden clubs nearby.

National parks and forests forbid the gathering of any plant part save ripe fruit about to fall off the bough. The wild plant enthusiast may collect ripe seed only—no cuttings, no rootstock—from these public areas, therefore. Local public parks and woodlands, even private wilderness areas, may post similar warnings. Even if they don't, common sense dictates that in any area where wild plants thrive for the purpose of entertaining, educating, exposing large numbers of people to their native habits, wild plant foragers should forbear. The old argument of "If everybody did . . ." holds true here.

Which leaves us with private property. Now, some conservationists would argue that even on private property, even with the owner's approval, wild plants should not be moved. Their position is too precarious in the world, these people would claim, and any disturbance to one plant community disturbs the population as a whole. I would answer that in comparison with other enterprises of human culture, the occasional gathering of wild plants does not threaten the plant world, *if* (1) the plant hunter is well informed of endangered species, (2) the property owner has agreed to the plan, and (3) the transplantation is done in a way that respects the growing habits of the plant and its community.

At the request of Congress, the Smithsonian Institution published a list of endangered plant species in 1978. The list is nationwide and small, considering the thousands of species native to the United States. Furthermore, the only regulations attached to the list prohibit plant gathering for commercial trade, not individual study. The Smithsonian list is a start, but it's not the final word on plants so endangered that we should avoid gathering them.

State lists and laws come closer to that need, and the avid wild plant gatherer must conscientiously ask about her own state's list of endangered plant species. In my home state of Virginia, for example, the Cooperative Extension Service publishes a list of "Native Plants Needing Protection," which does not prohibit their gathering but discourages their use for decorative purposes other than growing them in a garden or nursery. Likewise Arkansas's Natural Heritage Commission publishes a list of what it calls "special plants" not legally endangered, but rare enough to deserve the care and attention of all of us concerned with prolonging all species found in the wild. New York State publishes a list of protected native plants, but state law there goes only so far as to prohibit gathering those plants on state property and to require permission of the owner before gathering on private property—a matter of common courtesy, state law or not. Most states in the desert Southwest have recently enacted tough laws, particularly designed to stop the threat of cactus rustling. More than two hundred cacti appear on the Arizona list, for instance, and the penalties for digging them up are stiff: $1,000 and up to eighteen months in jail.

The preservation of endangered species is serious business. This concern must be shared by those who gather wild plants for their windowsill right alongside the stricter conservationists who would discourage any gathering whatsoever. Perhaps through educated study and observation we foragers can earn the reputation of being as conscientious and knowledgeable about wild plants as those who wander the woods without touching. Then we can join together in the effort to save the plants that the world might altogether lose.

Going Out Ready

One way to shoulder your responsibility as a steward of the wild is by making sure that the plants you do adopt make it home alive. You can't very well decide in the midst of a walk in the woods that you want to gather seeds or cuttings. You have to go out ready to gather, with the proper equipment at hand.

For gathering living plants, a bucket and trowel are imperative. The size of each depends, of course, on the size of the plants you are gathering. Often a plastic gallon milk jug, trimmed to include the handle but not the cap, serves as a handy container to carry along in a knapsack. Larger plants may need a five-gallon bucket, and they may also require a shovel of larger size. Gloves are handy, as is a jackknife or clippers to trim and prune. An extra cup often helps, so you can scoop water up out of a lake or stream to soak in around plant roots for the journey home.

Gathering wild seed requires different equipment, but again your needs will be dictated by the plants you seek. I have found that for many small-seeded plants ordinary stationery envelopes work very well. Gather a handful of seed, or even tip the seed head into the envelope and tap the seeds off into it. You can easily carry several envelopes, to collect different kinds of seed, and you can also store the seed in those envelopes if you don't want to sprout them immediately.

I list these rules so dogmatically. But many's the time I've wrapped a little plant in sycamore leaves or corn shucks from the field, since I'd gone out for an aimless walk, not knowing I'd do any gathering. Wild plants pop up everywhere; gathering them to grow indoors is an adventure born of curiosity, a curiosity that never fades. As important as the equipment carried with you is that spirit: the love of the wild.

Wild Beauties on the Windowsill

Despite occasional pragmatic usefulness, houseplants primarily beautify a home. Their draping curves offset sharp corners. Their brilliant greens contrast with decorator colors, with white walls, with wood. Their chaotic cascades of leaf, stalk, and vine subtly mock the orderliness of a place for everything, everything in its place in the household regime. In a tidy household, houseplants emphasize the randomness of nature. In a cluttered household, houseplants stand serene and unencumbered. They're living things. They depend on their keepers; they reflect their owners, just like cats and dogs. Healthy houseplants enhance any living space like clean air, sunshine, good music.

The beauty of wild plants, more than any other feature, makes them appropriate to bring indoors. We're not all that used to singling out a wild plant from among the tangle of weeds and regarding it with that eye for design that we regularly cast on houseplants. Some don't stand up to that kind of scrutiny, but others do.

Some, when separated from the mass of green that supports them, will spread low and drape amply and seem to enjoy their autonomy. Others will continue to try to grow straight up, skinny and tall. Unless they're potted in with other plants, they won't pass the test for beauty. I've rejected plenty of plants on purely aesthetic grounds, even though they survived through potting. Yet others I found, much to my surprise, gained interest to my eyes once removed from a weedy environment and placed on windowsill display.

SAPONARIA

(Saponaria officinalis)

A surprisingly graceful plant, tolerant of indoor conditions and eager to grow all year round, is the saponaria. Often dubbed with the cheerful nickname bouncing bet, its white or pink five-petaled flowers bounce their way through summer, filling in fields, lining roadways, practically everywhere across the continent. Another nickname given this plant is soapwort, harking back to an earlier era when the high concentration of saponins, naturally occurring soapy stuff within the plant's cells themselves, made saponaria a ready source for suds. Colonial gardens would have included a corner filled with saponaria, for it was used to wash skin and fabrics. Even today, fabric conservators turn to saponaria to cleanse fine tapestries and aged cloth that might be damaged by modern detergents.

Saponaria is a perennial. In spring its woody rootstock sprouts unassuming greenery. Summer sees the stalks extend up and branch out. Smooth oval leaves, quite a dark green, grow in pairs opposite one another off the slender stalk. A noticeable node marks each point where leaves contact stalk. By midsummer, from the tip of each growing stalk, a cluster of flowers opens to the sun, pink in color or so light pink as to appear white. Sturdy flowers, they'll bloom in the wild through the summer, until they close up on the forming seeds, scattered at frost time to make new plants next year.

Saponaria is quite easy to adopt at any period during its growing season. If you can identify it before it begins to flower, you may bring it in and watch it offer blooms to you. But if you find it in flower, you can easily clip it back and bring it in just the same. Given adequate lighting, it will get back to work producing flowers within two weeks.

You'll find that saponaria grows from a relatively shallow network of slender woody roots, similar in shape and noded character to the aboveground stalks. Since saponaria grows in clusters, it is relatively easy to dig up a cluster of plants ample to fill a middle-size pot. Saponaria is hardy enough to withstand your stripping its rootstock of the hard wild soil in which it stands. If you don't linger, you can take naked sprigs home to root. Prepare the standard wild plant potting soil mix, and set in the roots about three inches under the soil level, probably an inch below the level at which they grew outside.

With those pronounced nodes and its hardy way of growing, saponaria presents a good plant to slip-root, too. Avoid flowering branches if you want to root a slip of saponaria. Find a leafy stalk originating near the base of the plant. Cut with a sharp knife, making a clean diagonal slice as close to the ground as convenient, resulting in a slip six to eight inches long or more. Your slip must have at least five nodes, because you have to strip the first two nodes of leaves and set them into the rooting medium. You'll want at least three left aboveground for the start of your saponaria plant.

Vermiculite or perlite is probably the best medium for rooting cuttings. If your cutting came out ragged, give it a sharp clean edge when you bring it inside. Let it sit half an hour to heal over, then dust with a rooting booster like commercially available Rootone.

In the meantime, prepare a pot for the purpose. Plastic pots work best, since the rooting medium must be kept moist at all times. Fill the pot with your chosen medium, then moisten thoroughly by pouring enough water into the pot that it runs out the drainhole. Tamp down to avoid air pockets, then use a pencil or knitting needle to make thin holes into which you can put your slips. Insert each cutting, making sure that two nodes, stripped of leaves, stay beneath soil level, then pack the rooting medium in around the cutting very well. The contact between the rooting medium and the noded stalk is essential. Only if the plant cells at the node sense that a growing medium and moisture await will they slowly multiply outward, sending rootlets out in search of water and support.

You may want to create a miniature greenhouse around your saponaria slips by puffing out a plastic bag, encircling the pot with it, and sealing it with a rubber band or tightly tied string. This mini-environment will rarely need watering. Keep an eye on it anyway, to prevent mold or algae from taking over. Root cuttings away from the window; root growth does not need sun.

In two to three weeks you should enjoy success with slips of saponaria. Give one a gentle tug. If it resists, it has probably grown roots down under. Once the roots have taken off, it's time to repot the plants in a soil medium, start fertilizing them regularly along with other growing plants, and set them in a brighter position.

Bright sunshine in the wild keeps saponaria standing upright, at least a foot tall. But the reduced light it gets on a windowsill or under a grow-light seems to encourage draping. Larger, heavier stalks swoop down out of the pot, their growing ends turning up to meet the light. Light less intense than that of the bright midsummer sun may evoke fewer and paler flowers, or no flowers at all. But I find that the saponaria, with its deep-green, smooth, oval leaves and its gentle curving patterns, makes a lovely foliage plant all winter long.

If you're curious to experience the soapy qualities of saponaria, and you're ready to sacrifice a handful of leaves for the cause, try this experiment. Take a handful of leaves and one or two healthy tufts of greenery, crush them under running water, and rub them together as if they were a bar of soap. You should see, sudsing up before your eyes, little green bubbles of saponaria foam. It's got a pleasant smell, soapy and herby all at once.

One caution, however. Large quantities of saponaria, if ingested, could be harmful. The very chemical that sudses up like that could do damage to the digestive tract. Keep saponaria growing in a place where small children cannot reach it.

G R O U N D   I V Y

(Glechoma hederacea)

Ground ivy's a pleasant bitter mint that fills in shady spots in yards and orchards. You know it when you step on it. Its acrid scent perfumes the air. In early spring, one of the first-found flowers is the lavender ground ivy bloom. Like other mint flowers, although more visible for its good size, it's shaped like a lipped trumpet, with frills as it fans out.

Ground ivy takes to potting quite comfortably. Since it weathers cold weather (though it disappears in a freeze), you can gather it in autumn or in early spring and enjoy its greens and blooms indoors.

You'll find that ground ivy clings to the ground with a shallow, fibrous root system, easily pulled up, even by hand. Branches creep along the ground from a rooted center, setting down more roots from each adjacent node. You don't have to dig too deep to come up with a ball of dirt securing ground ivy roots. Use a small- to medium-size pot, made of either clay or plastic, and filled with the standard wild plant potting soil. Ground ivy doesn't require that much special care.

As the weeks roll on and your ground ivy gets established, graceful trailing stalks will curl over the pot edge. This trailing shape makes ground ivy a fine plant to place in a hanging pot or basket.

Naturally, ground ivy chooses shady places, so it really doesn't need much sun. The first ground ivy I got to know, I remember, spread out under two large Chinese chestnut trees, protected from direct light by their spreading branches. Put your ground ivy in a morning- or evening-light window, eastern or western exposure, and it should do very well.

It will bloom in season with its outdoor counterparts, in early spring—March, perhaps in April—then provide handsome foliage throughout the year. Water it only when the soil feels dry to the touch. Ground ivy's a good one to get started with. It's easy to grow and pretty to see.

P L A N T A I N

(Plantago major)

Broadleaf plantain is a large leafy plant, so common that even if you haven't made a point of finding it, you've probably stepped right over it many a time. Parallel veins run the length of its wide, oval, smooth-edged leaves. It finds its way into backyards, gardens, city lots, even through cracks in the sidewalk, as well as along the edge of country roads. It grows low to the ground, so it favors those places where other plants give it room to stretch out its leaves.

Find a plantain, and you learn that this annual plant grows numerous leaves from a single center. From that same center shoots a network of stringy roots, as extensive in their reach as the leaves. A hardy plant, it's

easily uprooted for transplantation, but be choosy as you select one to bring home. Good soil and sun conditions can make for a healthy, bushy plantain; in adverse conditions, a plantain grows on, but remains scrawny and unattractive. Needless to say, you'll want to gather the former.

I found a plantain I couldn't resist gathering from my garden. The nitrogen-rich soil I'd provided for the vegetables suited the plantain as well. It was a beautiful plant, one of the healthiest I have seen, with leaves as wide and long as my hand, crisp like a new head of lettuce. I gave it a windowsill home in a seven-inch plastic pot full of standard wild plant potting soil, and it spent a pleasant growing season with me.

Plantains do need plenty of water. Even in a soil designed to retain water, even set into a plastic pot, that plantain tended to wilt on a hot summer day unless I watered it once, sometimes even twice a day.

And plantains do need plenty of light. *Au naturel*, plantain chooses a sunny location, but it will sprout and maintain itself in the shade as well. Likewise, an adopted plantain may succeed in an eastern or western exposure, but it will prefer the sunniest window or porch you've got. But even if grown in partial light inside, plantain will shoot up its flowerstalk in midsummer. A curious-looking, long, skinny stalk, it will snake up in among the bushy leaves, adding interest to the design of your plant. You may choose to snip these stalks, because their development may diminish that of the leaves. But their shape is so intriguing you may just choose to let them be, as I do.

Plantain is edible. It has its own bland, green taste. People gather it to add to salads, picking the innermost tender leaves. It's used medicinally as well, commonly called Indian Band-Aid because of its mildly astringent juice.

And now we have found another value for the plantain, so often stepped on, pulled up, ignored as a weed. Take it out of its context, pot it on the windowsill, lo and behold! Plantain becomes a thing of beauty, not just a lowly weed.

MOUNTAIN LAUREL

(Kalmia latifolia)

Mountain laurel is a handsome, slow-growing evergreen shrub. Brought indoors, it won't grow fast and it probably won't bloom. But it's a dependable, substantial foliage gathering, ranging in size from six inches up to six feet. Of course, the larger the plant you gather, the bigger risk you take in transplanting. But you can bring in a little mountain laurel with a minimum of trouble, and you can keep it growing green and shiny with a minimum of work as well.

Of course, you've got to start out knowing where to find mountain laurel. It won't be found in the prairie plains. As the name makes clear, it's a mountain lover, but you don't have to brave the heights to find it. It ranges throughout the eastern United States, spreading down the mountains running from Georgia to Maine and into the forested foothills surrounding.

A mountain laurel thicket has a distinctive shape. Gnarled trunks curl over, forming woodland arcs. A mountain laurel grove seems scaled for little people. Its evergreen leaves shine deep green even as winter reigns, and although its own growing seasons do not proceed as dramatically as those of deciduous trees, the dormant period between fall and spring is the best time to select a mountain laurel plant to bring home.

These shrubs grow from woody rootstock, apparently unhindered by the abundance of rocks and roots in the forest soil. If you set about digging out a large mountain laurel, you've got a job on your hands. Dig a trench one to two feet away from the base of the trunk, so that you unearth a ball of soil and substantial roots to sustain the plant. A smaller shrub requires less digging.

You can tell that the mountain laurel chooses a rich forest soil, so it requires the same enrichment at home. A high-humus potting soil mix does best for a mountain laurel. Perhaps the easiest recipe calls for one part standard wild plant potting soil enriched with one part peat moss or humus. Thoroughly moisten the soil as you set the plant's roots down into it, but thereafter water only infrequently.

You may find with mountain laurel, as with many other wild plants you bring indoors, that it will shed leaves during the first few weeks on your windowsill. You need to be alarmed only if it sheds every leaf and puts out no new ones. Then your plant is in trouble. But if a few drop here or there and then a few new ones sprout again, it's a sign your plant is getting used to its new surroundings and you're caring well for it.

Mountain laurel is not fussy about light conditions, although a brighter window spot may encourage further growing. A full-sun indoor location—not even equal to the brilliance of a shady forest glen—may even bring on a small cluster of red and white spring flowers. But don't expect a bloom as abundant as the one you see in the woods.

If you've gathered the mountain laurel to enjoy its foliage only, maintain its luster with a regular monthly fertilizing routine. If, on the other hand, you can give it the ample diffuse light it needs—in other words, if you've got a porch or sunroom where springtime light falls on it more than half the day—fertilize more sparingly. A regular dose of plant food two weeks after you pot it up, then once a month through summer and autumn and none through winter into spring, should boost flower production.

Since the leathery laurel leaves collect dust, they'll do well with an occasional polish. Just dampen a soft cloth, using a little gentle soap in the water if the dust is thick. Mountain laurels also like misting.

One warning: Don't eat the mountain laurel. Not that I imagine *you* would try, but adventuresome toddlers might. Botanical relations to our woodland *Kalmia latifolia* were singled out by the wild maenads famed for their Bacchanalian rites. They ate the laurel leaves to bring on a frenzy. Goats I've seen who have eaten mountain laurel become tipsy, grind their teeth, and spit up green straw; clearly they don't feel good. I wouldn't want to go through it myself, and any householder growing an indoor mountain laurel plant must be forewarned of this hazard.

Y U C C A

(Yucca filamentosa)

Surely some people will roll their eyes when you say you're gathering yucca plants to grow in pots indoors.

"Yucca? That weed? Help yourself!" I can just hear them saying.

Even as far north as my home state of Virginia, yuccas spread rapaciously. They originally grew in the dry desert regions far southwest of us. Some people transported them here as ornamentals. They tolerate the dry heat and the frost, and they send up magnificent flowerstalks. I know fields scattered with tough fibrous yuccas, where the fist-size seedpods have matured and opened and the dime-size seeds have sprouted into new plants, neither cultivated nor controlled nor even wanted.

Any plant with leaves that tough must grow from a sizable root. In fact, it's hard to get a glimpse of the entire root of a full-size yucca, unless you begin by digging a foot away from the crown of the plant and dig a ditch three feet deep all around it. Then maybe, maybe you'll see how the taproot delves down underground, big around as your wrist, and splits off to explore the depths where few other neighboring plant roots reach. Chances are your shovel will snap a rootlet here or there. Don't worry. Yucca will endure it.

In fact, you don't really have to dig such a large hole in order to unearth and safely gather a growing yucca plant. I've done it quite haphazardly, and the yucca still survived. Its survival mechanism might not be geared for just this sort of abuse, but the panoply of abuses it is ready to survive makes it able to survive this one.

To be safe, and kind to the yucca, you should go out ready to dig with a good strong shovel. Shove it in at least six inches from the yucca's crown, and make a circle of slices all around it. That should take you at least a foot underground, so that even if now you slice the yucca's taproot, it will have something to grow from.

Slice through that root, and you can already sense how fibrous it grows. The outside of the root is dirt-brown, almost red, but the inner core is bright white and composed of tough, ropelike strands. The root is high in saponins—plant-produced soap—and has been used by Indians and herbalists as a source for a gentle nondetergent hair wash.

Even a foot-deep yucca taproot will have some threadlike rootlets emanating from it. Give it a rich soil and a little moisture to settle in with, and that stub of a taproot will start sprouting more little roots. It's the tiny root hairs waving through the soil that send water and nutrients up into the root, the leaves, the flowers. The taproot is a major channel, but it doesn't collect much water itself. So the first week or so of potted growth is crucial to the yucca, as it develops a new network of water-conducting rootlets through the soil. Obviously, you'll need a big pot for a yucca. Give that taproot plenty of room, plenty of soil, plenty of opportunity to sprout a supporting root system.

But since the plant is originally a desert plant, you need to worry less in the case of yucca about porosity of soil and drainage in the pot. This is one wild plant you can set into that beautiful handmade glazed ceramic pot with no holes in the bottom. Don't take this proviso to mean that you can waterlog the plant. Overwatering would cause the root to rot, the leaves to yellow and sag. On the contrary, water your yucca less than most other wildflowers.

Concoct a mixture of wild plant potting soil and begin by layering rock or perlite on the bottom one inch deep. Then fill to a depth of two to three inches above the rock or perlite with the soil. Set the yucca in, being aware of its angle. A crooked yucca plant, set in the pot wrong, probably won't right itself for a long, long time, and along the way it will look silly.

Then sprinkle in soil all around the rest of the root, bringing the soil level up to the former soil level, where the leaf structure rises up. Water adequately. If you have used a pot without drainage, though, water your yucca one cup at a time. When the soil on top feels moist, stop. Water sparingly, and only when the soil feels dry to the touch, from now on.

Your yucca plant might register some discomfort at being ripped from its outdoor home, deprived of a full-size root. A leaf here or there may yellow or brown, indicating that new passages of water transport have not fully been established. Many plants experience this weakening during transplanting, but with good treatment they will pull through. Don't overwater, and give the yucca moderate lighting for the first two weeks. After that point, you can trim off damaged leaves and increase your lighting, if desired.

In the wild, yucca grows in open sunlight and full-day sunlight brings on its bloom. Most household situations will not, therefore, allow the yucca to achieve flowering. Yet it will manage quite happily to stay green and lively, making a large, distinctive houseplant that will tolerate the light offered by a western or eastern window. Too little light may cause it to dwindle, but slowly, perhaps imperceptibly, over months. This plant has learned to tolerate extremes of hot and cold, but if it had its way it would seek out strong light.

But yuccas have over the centuries endured many hardships—brick-hard soil, months without water, the unabated desert sun. Being potted and put inside might just feel like pampering to a yucca, and it will grow large and carefree in a loving home.

PIGGYBACK PLANT

(Tolmiea menziesii)

If you're an avid houseplant grower, even if you don't live near the forests of the Northwest coastline, you probably already know this cunning little plant. It's a popular, easy-to-grow, commercially available houseplant. With a minimum of trouble, it grows on a sunny windowsill. But its native homelands are the deep fir woods of Washington and Oregon,

making it one of the few common commercial houseplants native to the northern hemisphere. Its botanical name commemorates its New-World identity, for it was named after Dr. William Tolmie, a surgeon for the Hudson Bay Company. If you're lucky enough to linger in those woods for a while, you'll have the pleasure of seeing this plant as it wishes to be seen: in slant light sifting through leaves and needles, in secluded corners of the Northwest's forest floor.

The piggyback is a small plant, tender and delicate. Its leaves are almost furry to the touch. A fibrous network of slender roots pokes down among roots and rocks. It supports a cluster of light-green leaves, shaped something like the maple leaf, which rarely grow to the size of a human hand. In the best of conditions, a dozen or more of these leaves will cluster, creating a fuzzy green bouquet.

All plants strive to reproduce their kind, but the piggyback does so quite unconventionally. From the point at which stem meets leaf spring little mini-piggybacks, identical in form but minuscule in size, a little plant within a plant. In its native habitat, the more mature piggyback leaves retire and recline onto fertile ground. Once contact is established

---

between soil and plant, roots grow out under the sprouting new plantlet. That's how colonies of piggyback plants begin. With each new turn of the piggyback generations, older plants spread ever outward, creating ever more of their kind.

But piggybacks don't need a native environment to play this trick, as many houseplant lovers know already. Indeed, often those little mini-piggybacks develop on a healthy plant's primary leaves without a bed of soil beneath them. But tip those large leaves down into soil, even clip them off the parent plant, and they will sprout new piggybacks soon. Successful growers can watch many a piggyback come to be.

You can also use this regenerative method to gather a piggyback plant for home without unearthing any. Clip a large leaf from a plant in the wild, particularly one already sprouting new plants at its center. Carry it home either in a plastic bag or tipped into moist soil, being careful not to bend or bruise it. Once home, trim off all but an inch of the major leaf-stalk, then press the growing center of the leaf and its offspring about half an inch down into a pot of moistened wild plant potting soil. A pebble placed on the leafstalk remaining will anchor the plant down to the medium you wish it to adapt to. Be sure that the soil remains moist but never waterlogged, and in a matter of weeks that plant will have set down roots and found a home.

Gather them from the wild, and you'll notice that the piggyback prefers the rich, dark soil and hazy filtered light of an evergreen forest. Our wild plant potting soil will do well to provide it with nutritious soil and water-retentive material all in one recipe. A single piggyback plant doesn't grow very large, so a six-inch pot will hold it well. But if you wish to see the piggyback sprout new kindred as it does in the wild, set it into a wide yet shallow planting tub where it can lay its leaves down flat alongside. Water only when the soil is dry to the touch; mist it occasionally, but not in midday when the sun would scorch the leaves. Moderate to full daylight will keep the piggyback plant happy. Too much sunlight could be worse for it than too little.

Of all the plants in the book, this one's the one least likely to set people spinning as they reconsider what houseplants might be. But perhaps, then, I can claim this plant as the proverbial exception that proves my rule. Here's a wild plant that's already been singled out as a houseplant *par excellence*. If you hadn't seen it sold in the plant shop, you'd probably be laughing about growing this weed indoors, too.

V I N C A

(Vinca minor)

The same qualities that make vinca a popular outdoor groundcover make it a successful indoor houseplant. It's pretty—dark and shiny. It's evergreen. It doesn't require special treatment, needs no special soils to support it. And it blooms a delicate pastel-blue flower early in the spring.

Strictly speaking, vinca isn't a wildflower. It was brought to this continent by Europeans as a handsome garden creeper. Many's the old homesite, aged graveyard, or overrun embankment still glistening with vinca all through the year. It may once have been planted, but now it has all but gone wild. It holds on tight and does well for itself even if abandoned by its planters.

If you go out to dig up vinca, you might not know where to begin.

Strands of green spread here and there, leafing out, then setting down roots again from a leafstalk node, forming a network anchored down every ten or twelve inches. Begin by digging in under the mature vine where the leaves grow thick and several stalks branch out. You may have to tug some rootlets out, but you'll come up with a flowing bunch of green. Some branches stay short and leafy. Others spread long and thin. Depending on whether you want your houseplant stout or draping, you can leave the tendrils hanging or cut them as you wish.

If you're gathering vinca from a full-grown patch, you'll probably notice that each flowing tendril has rooted or tried to root from several different nodes. By means of this growing habit, vinca manages to spread, making it a good groundcover. With each new season of greenery, it spreads out rooting potential as well. To be sure you transplant a plant that will make it, look for a sprig of vinca fully rooted, not a node that's setting out new roots from up above.

Depending on what time of year you gather a plant of vinca, you may enjoy it as a green houseplant or as a windowsill bloom. To assure that handsome light-blue bloom, gather a late-winter vinca and force it. Since the plant is evergreen, you'll never have trouble finding it unless it's covered with snow. And even then, if you remember where the vinca grows and are feeling intrepid about gathering, you could probably adopt a vinca from under the snow. All that might stop you is earth frozen solid.

Although vinca doesn't show the signs of wilting that so many other wild plants show when you dig them up, it's still a good idea to respect its daily cycle and gather it in the morning or evening, not in the midday sun. Set it into a pot of wild plant potting soil. With roots so slight, you have to take care to sprinkle more soil in around them, tamping it over them gently to assure a good seal.

Put the vinca at any sunny springtime windowsill—east, south, or west in exposure. A springtime bloomer, vinca responds to short days of light, blooming naturally under spring shadows cast by evergreen trees and shrubs. In fact, if anything, you ought to worry about giving it too much light. You will have to observe the plant in your own environment, notice whether the flower bud perks up, notice whether it retains most of its leaves, to see whether the windowsill home you've given it provides your vinca with what it needs.

And then will come the day when that lovely pale-blue blossom spins open. Most vinca plants send up only one flowerstalk, so if you are hoping for abundant vinca in bloom, begin by gathering plants in abundance. If a single, simple blossom will satisfy you, a little pot with two or three vinca sprouts should more than suffice.

The flower will stay open for about a week; then it will dwindle. But the vinca in leaf, with its glossy green and its graceful twining, still offers attractive windowsill foliage that will last all summer, through the winter, until another season of vinca in bloom.

Vinca's a good one to start with if you're not so sure about potting up weeds. It often grows nearby; no need to tramp out in the woods looking. Its needs are few; it requires little pampering. It fulfills most people's expectations of a pleasant houseplant: graceful, growing, and green.

V I O L E T S

(Viola spp.)

Violets remind everyone of spring. Those tender flowers couldn't bear the hot summer sun. They choose to bloom when the surrounding grass and weeds have barely awakened, when the vernal sun slants through blossoming fruit trees and velvety newborn leaves.

Just as they need nature's springtime to enjoy a full-fledged blooming, they'll need a sense of the seasons when you bring them indoors. Violets are one of those many wild things that require winter dormancy, but in return for your patience, they'll offer the lift of an early-spring blooming on your windowsill.

Dig up a common blue violet, *Viola papilionacea,* common to the East Coast; if you live in the West, try the yellow stream violet, *Viola glabella,* common to the West Coast. You will discover that these diminutive plants grow out of a fat, finger-size rhizome running not too deep under-

---

ground. The rhizome serves as a storage unit during hibernation, collecting sugars manufactured by the leaves during the months after blooming, ready to spring forth at another growing season.

Needless to say, the tubers are essential to a potted gathering of wild violets. I have found that even if I wish to gather a summer potful of violets for their foliage alone, they shrink back, leaving me with a potful of leafless tubers in only a matter of weeks. To get around this frustration, I decided to gather violet tubers at the end of their growing cycle, when I had no expectation of foliage until the next spring. The plan worked.

It was late November when I set the tubers of common blue violet, ten of them, into a seven-inch clay pot filled with my wild plant potting soil. I tucked them into the soil at the same depth at which I found them—not more than an inch under the surface. I watered the soil thoroughly, letting it drain through the hole at the pot's bottom. Then I slipped over the pot a clear plastic bag, sealing it around the edges with a rubber band. I kept the sealed pot of violets at the edge of an east-facing window, where it received moderate indirect sunlight. The soil stayed moist and encouraged a few leafy sprouts, but violet activity stayed at a minimum.

The plastic bag fulfilled other purposes. I went on a two-week vacation, and it allowed me to leave without worry that the violets would dry

up. Those juicy tubers need some moisture surrounding them, even when the plant lies dormant, and putting a plastic bag around the pot left the violet project more carefree. I removed the plastic and checked the soil for moisture and the threat of mold occasionally over the winter. Still just two or three minuscule leaves braved the light of day, and otherwise my potted violet remained unseen.

It must have been mid-February when signs of life returned. Lo and behold, pushing through under that clear plastic wrap were twelve or fifteen fresh new violet leaves, healthy and green as could be. Time to take the plastic off and let the violet breathe the air, feel the sunshine, let it think it's spring. Soon enough, violet flowers started poking up on their own little stalks, and for two full weeks during a snowy February I had a springtime pot of violets blooming on my windowsill.

I suppose some people think it's crazy to spend a whole winter waiting for two weeks of violet blooms. But the pleasure gained from that early-spring potful of purple more than repaid me for the time spent waiting for the blooms. And it certainly didn't take much work to wait. Looking back, I realize that the violets didn't even have to take space on my windowsill, in fact. So little leaf sprouting went on over the winter, they didn't need any sunlight to survive. Next winter I'll keep the pot in a closet or corner until spring sprouts appear, and my violets may even like it better that way.

Turns out I'm not the only one who has been growing violets under glass. Robert Baur, president of the Terrarium Association (57 Wolfpit Avenue, Norwalk, CT 06851), says that he plants a series of shallow forcing bowls full of violets before winter, enough to keep violets blooming indoors for three months straight. He prepares a bowl three to four inches deep with a layer of sphagnum moss, charcoal, and gravel, then over that he sifts a layer of soil. He tips in violet rhizomes so that the eyes atop them, from which leaves and flowers sprout, rise above the soil surface. He covers the bowls with a translucent cover, keeps the soil moist but not waterlogged, and keeps them in a window providing at least half-day sunshine. He says that once flower buds form, you can put the bowl into the refrigerator and hold onto them for weeks, until you want the violets to bloom. Take them out two days before Valentine's Day or Easter.

Now that spring is in full swing outside, violet blossoms dotting the yard, my indoor violet has moved on toward summer. *Now* I enjoy the rich greens of violet foliage. The little heart-shaped leaves never grow much taller than three or four inches, never droop, never dangle, never vine. They need a lot of water, so much that I decided to transplant them into a plastic pot. To some people's eyes, trained to the look of expectable house plants, a potted violet may seem silly. But these very violets, if allowed to fulfill their natural cycle of photosynthesis and decline, will come up blooming again some snowy day next February, promising that spring's not far behind.

C I N N A M O N   V I N E

(Dioscorea batatas)

When I first started this project, I was convinced that many wild things would take to water culture swimmingly. Honeysuckle, greenbrier, all those twining vines—I thought they would take off if I clipped them and stuck them in a glass of water.

I was wrong. Those twining weedy vines have stems too woody for water culture. Houseplants we are used to clipping and sticking in water are tropical, faster-growing, and more accustomed to higher moisture levels all around them, so the transition from soil to water culture doesn't give them so much of a shock.

The only curious exception I've found to this rule (not that I've exhausted every possibility) is the so-called cinnamon vine. This particular plant's response to water culture is curious, because it doesn't continue to grow leafy and green. The water triggers its panic mechanism, encouraging it to reproduce. And instead of making seeds, this wild plant makes what look like little potatoes.

The leaves are distinctive, so recognizable that they're the best way to spot the cinnamon vine. They are heart-shaped, sometimes tinged with red, almost as if embossed with veins that run parallel from the stem end to the tip end of the shiny leaf.

The vines twine through the summer months. Well-established leaves run to four, five inches long, while new leaves, identical in shape, measure only an inch long or less. I've seen the cinnamon vine in rather civilized places—twining up the shrubbery at the back door of a friend, overwhelming road cuts at an in-town location.

Here's how to get this plant to perform its trick for you. Find a strand that's twining to a length of at least a foot. Find several, if you can. Clip them neatly off and stick them into a tall vase full of water. If you want to keep up appearances, add a little chunk of charcoal to the water before you stick in the plant. It will discourage the accumulation of green algae and make the experiment look better, although otherwise it doesn't influence its success.

Now just wait. You can do other things as you're waiting, because it may take three, four weeks, even a month, before you realize that this pleasant-looking greenery is sprouting strange brown growths. From each available node, where heart-shaped leaf sprouts off from stem, small brown tuberlike excrescences are developing, just like little potatoes on the vine. They even have tiny eyes, just like little potatoes. No doubt if it had to, each little growth could sprout a whole new plant of this wild cinnamon vine.

There's a limit to the entertainment value of the cinnamon vine. Eventually, as if it were in the wild and having to see to survival, the plant sheds those little tubers and your fun is done. But it's an easy gathering, takes no care at all, and offers a glimpse into the plant world's everlasting will to survive.

W I L D   B E D S T R A W

(Galium spp.)

For a long time I hoped that wild bedstraw was sweet woodruff. I knew that the fine sandpaper leaves, in whorls of six or eight climbing the recumbent stalk, and the minute flowers growing at stalk's tip all could signal that identification. But every time I came upon the plant in our Appalachian woods, and now over the months that I have grown this tender herb in a pot, I keep giving it a pinch, hoping to smell the sweet scent of May wine. But no—it just smells grassy. Must be bedstraw.

I still enjoy growing this little wild plant on my windowsill. I find it in the wild very often, growing in clumps among woodland weeds, even along shorn banks, competing with ferns and grasses. When it gets its room, oddly enough, it stays compact. When it has to compete with others, it grows gangly. When placed in a pot, it fluffs up and overspreads the sides, but it stays a dainty size. It's a good plant to set into a large-scale terrarium and a good plant for a windowsill short on light.

Going out to gather, look once spring is here for a light-green cluster of stalks, deeply ribbed and haloed by a whorl of leaves every inch or two along it. A certain roughness can be felt in leaves and stalks, but nothing compared to its near relative, cleavers (*Galium aparine*). The plants grow very similarly, but cleavers sprawls, needs a brighter environment, and isn't half as pretty, so it's not as good a potted plant as wild bedstraw. Yellow bedstraw (*Galium verum*), also closely related, has more promise on the windowsill, especially considering its cheery yellow flowers, tiny though they may be.

The root system from which the little wild bedstraw plant springs is as delicate as its foliage. You'll find it selecting quite rich, loamy soil. Our wild plant potting soil provides its needs.

Wild bedstraw requires special handling, because it can wilt easily. Don't expect to be able to stick the plant in your pocket and carry it home with you. Sure, you can handle some of the tougher weeds this way, but wild bedstraw needs more coddling. Uproot it in a trowel full of soil to support it; tuck it in a jar or bucket, even sprinkle stream water on it if you can, to ensure a safe journey home.

Bedstraw will require special care at home as well. Its light requirements are minimal, but its need for water greatly exceeds that of many other wild potted plants. Forget to water it for a couple of days, and you'll probably come home to a dry and withered wild bedstraw. Light but thorough daily watering—enough to see that the water has penetrated through the soil and is coming out the pot at the bottom—will keep a bedstraw plant perky and green for months, even in a northern windowsill. This excessive need for water makes wild bedstraw a prime candidate for a terrarium plant, where moisture permeates the closed environment and leaves and roots stay a little damp all day. In a pot, regular spritzing with a spray of water, morning or evening (not midday), will also help to replicate conditions like the sheltered woodland environment that the wild bedstraw needs.

H E U C H E R A

(Heuchera americana)

American heuchera, also known as alumroot, will make for a pretty little houseplant. Its lightly variegated, delicately scalloped leaves may cluster in sixes or eights, but it will never outgrow a four-inch pot. It will remain a miniature forever.

Closely related to the piggyback plant, various other heuchera species can be found from coast to coast. A smooth-leaved heuchera grows in rich woodland shadows along the East Coast, then inland toward the

plains. A fuzzier-leaved variety, *Heuchera chlorantha* or green-tinted heuchera, grows farther to the west. Also on the West Coast can be found the striking poker heuchera (*H. cylindrica*), primarily found in Oregon, and the so-called jack o' the rocks (*H. rubescens*), found farther south, into the Mohave Desert. All the heucheras share a similar foliage pattern: ruffle-edged, maple-shaped leaves, one to a stalk, clustering from a single growing center, which emerges from the fine fibrous network of roots underneath.

Although related plants are cultivated outdoors for their pretty flowers, heuchera's windowsill potential runs to leaves instead. If you have a porch or balcony where the plant can sit in subdued yet full diffuse light, you may enjoy the creamy spike of poker flowers or the curious green flowers of the green-tinted or American heuchera. But if you're gathering heuchera for a windowsill environment, your best bet is to keep light levels low and actually discourage flower formation. That way, you've got the delicate foliage to look at, and the leaves won't be robbed of nutrients by a flower pressing through.

Although the common name "alumroot" suggests a medicinal history, in only one source so far do I find any account of this plant's use as a healing herb. A book recounting Shaker uses of herbs names one species as an astringent without bitterness, a useful remedy for children with sore throats and stuffy noses. As the name suggests, the root was gathered and boiled. Considering this plant's diminutive size, it must have taken quite a lot of gathering.

Those who go out to gather the plant for potting will observe a root system that is slight and shallow, composed of numerous tendrils striking out underground. A loose, rich soil, like our wild plant potting soil, provides the best contained environment for heuchera. Water thoroughly as soon as you set the plant in the pot. After that, compared to other wild plants potted, heuchera will not need that much attention. Weekly watering and an occasional spritz will keep it looking green.

Heucheras are annual herbs. They want to set seeds and go under. You won't be able to make a winter gathering in the East, but in midspring to early summer you'll find the occasional wild heuchera. Bring it into a potted environment, and it may enjoy a windowsill life a month or two beyond the turn of the seasons.

SPIDERWORT

(Tradescantia americana)

A lovely American wildflower, spiderwort is one of the more dependable indoor blooms I've found. Its slender leaves press up through moistened forest humus in springtime. By summer its cluster of abundant blossoms begins to unfold, but only in the morning sunlight and rarely more than one per stalk each day. Since each inflorescence can cradle up to fifty blossoms, the bloom of a spiderwort can last many weeks. Each morning another gentle purple flower opens. Each afternoon it shuts, almost seeming to turn away from the bright sun of the solstice overhead. But by the next dawning, another spiderwort blossom has opened to the day.

At least eight different spiderwort species find their niches in different parts of the United States. All share certain characteristics, since all are part of the genus *Tradescantia*. Slender stems and leaves with parallel venation, a three-petaled bloom in the blue to pink range, pronounced bulging nodes where each new leafstalk or flowerstalk originates, and a delicate, day-long, intricate flower characterize every variety of spiderwort we know.

The spiderwort flower has received a lot of public attention in the last few years, in light of antinuclear research and protests, and for an intriguing reason. Low-level radiation, difficult to detect in the air, seems to alter the color of certain portions of certain spiderwort flowers. Not all spiderworts show the change; laboratory preparation is necessary. But because of this curious ability to register radioactivity, spiderwort has become more of a household word.

It can become more of a household plant as well, because it takes very well to potting. It may be difficult to single out spiderwort among other wildflowers before it blooms. Its narrow, grasslike leaves sprout from fibrous perennial rootstock. It spreads by root division. If you saw some blooming spiderwort someplace last year, you can be sure to find it sprouting up again there this spring. If you're starting on a search for spiderwort unfamiliar with the plant, you'd best wait until its blooming season to make a sure identification.

Each three-petaled flower reveals a fascinating structure deep within. A dense fuzz of hairs surrounds the central flower parts. These hairs are attached to the stamen, the male part of the spiderwort flower, and make the flower parts more accessible to insect pollinators. Seen under a microscope, or even under a small loupe, these hairs show themselves to be a single chain of cells, strung together like a strand of beads, a most remarkable sight. It's the stamen hairs of certain spiderwort varieties that turn pink in a radioactive environment. They're fascinating to look at, even in the clean country air.

If you find your spiderwort in summertime bloom, you may still succeed in adopting it for your windowsill and coaxing it to continue to bloom at home. I'd suggest that you make very sure to gather a full-bloom spiderwort in the cool of the evening, even though the flowers

_____

have by then shut down. Mark the spot at midday, then return at dusk. Try very hard not to shock the plant: Dig up a hefty root ball, tap most of that dirt off, and pot it up promptly, water it thoroughly, and give it a trim. The fewer leaves the plant must support as it reestablishes its bearings, the more likely it will revive soon and start making flowers again.

From a plant that's sending up, say, half a dozen flowerstalks, clip back three or four of them. Maintain the plant's foliage, but trim it back by about a third. Pot the plant in an ample pot with good drainage, using our standard wild plant potting soil mix. Do not fertilize until after it has bloomed. Spiderwort blooms outdoors whether it's growing in sun or shade. Its native environment is the shady forest, but garden transplants don't seem to mind it brighter. A sunny window facing east, south, or west will offer good light for its blooming. Relatively low-intensity grow-lights will coax a bloom too. A north-facing window or a window blocked to the sun may not provide enough light, but it's still worth a try. Spiderwort seems a plant determined to bloom, whatever its circumstances.

Spiderwort also seems determined to follow its own clockworks. I gathered my plant in mid-October, long after it had spent its blooms. I hoped perhaps to force a winter blossom, but the plant malingered all winter long in semihibernation. It didn't die back completely as many wild plants will do, but it didn't look too sprightly. I watered it maybe once a month through its dormancy.

Then somehow summer got into its veins. I was keeping the grow-lights on over fifteen hours a day, closely replicating day length near the solstice. But curiously enough, the daily bloom cycle of the spiderwort set its own time clock, maybe responding to the light pouring in the window alongside my grow-light rig, maybe responding to some inward yearning.

I'd get up at seven and turn the grow-light on. My spiderwort would already be blooming. By midday, I'd notice, the spiderwort had closed its bloom, not to open another until the next day's dawn. It was quite pleasing to wake up to a blooming windowsill wildflower, and to know that rhythms learned in the wild were still at work deep within it.

Those of you who do indeed adopt a spiderwort for your sill may be curious about the names for this woodland creature. Two theories are offered for the origin of "spiderwort." One suggests that the stems' crooked joints resemble the uplifted legs of a spider. The other theory points to the fact that when a stalk is snapped, the sap spins out in a thin strand like the threads of a spider's web.

No one disputes the origin of the botanical name for this genus, however. *Tradescantia* comes from John Tradescant, court botanist for Charles I, who must have learned of various newfound plants sent back by explorers from the New World during the early seventeenth century. The royal gardeners must soon have discovered, as Americans did in the years to come, that spiderwort readily spreads in cultivated grounds. These days, abandoned herb and flower gardens prove just as happy hunting grounds for spiderwort as the woods in which it grows wild.

Tradescantia rewarded me in my search for wildflowers that will bloom indoors—a search central to the inspiration of this book, and a search that has taught me much more about the requirements of wildflowers thriving outdoors. I've had to readjust my expectations. Black-eyed Susans just won't bloom on the windowsill. But spiderwort will, I'm pleased to say, and it will keep on blooming for weeks on a windowsill if you treat it kindly.

SNAKEBERRY

(Duchesnea indica)

I've finally found a use for the snakeberry. It always looks so inviting. But as long as I was gathering wild plants for cooking, I had to leave it alone. That three-part leaflet resembles the wild strawberry so closely. Those berries poke out, so tempting and red. Many who go in search of wild strawberries too late in the season think they've made a find, until on closer examination they realize the plant has fooled them again— those are snakeberries or mock strawberries, not sweet strawberries at all. Call them what you will, they're no good for eating. But now I know they make a lovely wildflower for the windowsill.

Closely related to the strawberry, in fact, the snakeberry spreads in backyards, roadsides, and woodland edges. Its little yellow flowers begin to bloom as early as the wild strawberry's white ones, but they keep right on blooming long past the time that strawberries fruit. And snakeberry's bright-red fruits hold on longer than strawberries too—maybe because nobody eats them.

Since it likes a shady spot and rounds out well with prunings, the snakeberry makes a perfect windowsill house plant. Dig in around a snakeberry plant, and you'll find that (just like its relative, the strawberry) each plant grows a cluster of reddish-green leafstalks, each holding that three-part leaf. These stalks arise from a similar spreading network of stringy little roots. A single node joins stalk and roots at ground level. Snakeberries propagate by runners; they shoot out nodes along the length of them, from which may spring a whole new plant.

The runners make snakeberry a pretty hanging plant. Those attached to the plants you gather may not survive the transplant; in fact, it's best to cut off runners when you pot the plants back home. But soon new runners will develop, overflowing your container, draping green abundantly along the windowsill.

The runners also make snakeberry a fun plant for kids who like to experiment. Those stringy little runners you clip off as you pot up snakeberry have the potential to form new plants, revealing the wondrous powers of plants to prolong their species. All your crew of naturalists needs is an aluminum pie plate filled with rooting medium—one part soil to two parts perlite. Moisten this soil, then lay the runners down on top of it. No need to set the runner into the soil, but you will need to set small rocks over each of the nodes along the runner to assure contact between plant and soil. If you water it (making sure not to overwater; holes in the pie plate's bottom will help), within a week little snakeberry plants will poke out from under those rocks. By the time three sets of leaves appear, the plant is ready for its own pot, this time a bit deeper, filled with a wild plant potting soil mix. Your children will have learned not only how a plant gets started but also how we can help it grow.

And in the meantime, a few full-grown snakeberry plants brought in from the wild, set in a six-to-eight-inch pot filled with standard wild plant potting soil, will begin to spread out and fill in the spaces on your windowsill. Given only moderate lighting, your snakeberry plant will soon bloom cheery yellow flowers, then set bright-red berries on the windowsill. Properly handled, in fact, the windowsill snakeberry should go on bearing even when outside temperatures drop, a festive Christmas plant in reds and greens to make the holiday decor a little bit wilder.

C L O V E R

(*Trifolium* spp.)

I don't know why, but I have a way of finding four-leaf clovers. Sometimes a feeling just comes over me; I look down, and there's a four-leaf underfoot. It can hapen three, four times in a walk through the fields. It can happen time and again in my own backyard.

At first, like everyone else, I considered it good luck. But now it's become second nature. And I realize it's a function not of intrinsic good luck, but of my constant habit of looking down, looking at plants in detail, seeing forms among the green. As my friend Lella Russell Smith put it, maybe it's the same way with good luck—there's a lot of it out there, but most people don't look often enough.

Because of this preoccupation with cloverly quaternities, I knew that

the clover plant I potted had to be a winner, too. I knew, from repeated observation, that more-than-three-leaf clover plants often sprout multiple good-luck charms. Find one sprig of four-leaf clover; look closer, and you're bound to find more four-leafs right nearby. So I was curious to see what would happen if I adopted a four-leaf clover plant for my windowsill.

I found the plant. A big, luscious red clover (*Trifolium pratense*), foliage only, no flower, with two great big good-luck four-leaf stalks.

Technically speaking, a lucky clover has four leaflets, each foursome constituting a leaf, each growing on a grassy stalk from the plant's center. The red clover leafstalk wraps around each leaf-bearing stem with a characteristic somewhat veiny sheath. If you gather the plant before blooming season—probably the best time to do so—it may seem just like a cluster of stems and leaves emerging from the ground.

The root system of a red clover is dense and fibrous, but not very deep. Red clover roots are among the most pronounced in their demonstration of the habit of many leguminous plants to develop a colony of bacteria on their roots. You can often see them—those little white nodules, the size of a pinhead or smaller, seeming to cling to the roots in a symbiotic relationship good for all concerned. The bacteria, called *Rhizobium*, seem to gain nourishment from the plant host. And by the same token, they fix nitrogen from the air, providing host plants with an essential nutrient that otherwise must be drawn from decaying organic matter. Farmers actually inoculate legume seeds with *Rhizobium* bacteria in order to foster this relationship and guarantee healthy green plants.

Tip a young red clover into a pot full of wild plant potting soil, give it a good watering to get it settled, and see it grow. Given moderate to full lighting, it will content itself on a windowsill all year round. It may shed a few leaves while getting used to new surroundings, but I found that my wild red clover did very well, even through winter, under grow-lights, since my eastern exposure didn't give it all the light it needed to keep on.

Other clovers should do as well, since red clover is among the larger of the clovers and would take more support than, say, a white or little hop clover. But taller varieties, like sweet clover (melilot) or alfalfa, may feel stunted in a pot and not do well at all. And from red clover, I'm afraid we can't expect an indoors bloom. It needs the full summer sunshine to support that heavy blossom.

But we can, I've discovered, expect a continuation of four-leaf growth. My plant proved an interesting experiment. For the first two months after I potted it, it reverted to sending out three-leaf foliage. The two four-leaf stalks it had when I gathered it were among the leaves that shed. I thought, shucks, can't grow a four-leaf clover indoors.

But I kept it watered, only when dry to the touch. I fertilized it monthly. I grew it under my grow-light rig, coaxed it along with feeling.

Seems that it took a couple of months to get settled in, then it went to town—four-leaf clovers, five-leaf clovers galore. Once it started shooting up strong new growth, it started making more-than-three-leafs again. And it keeps on making them, now and then, giving me good luck in among my other windowsill wildflowers.

CHAPTER 3

Wild Garden on the Windowsill

A windowsill wild garden can have its practical purposes too. Numerous common wild things are edible and tasty, and some of them adapt to indoor cultivation well. Just as it may take some minor adjustments of expectation to accustom oneself to potted wildflowers, with the same subtle shifts in taste wild plants become suitable garnishes, if not entrées in even a gourmet cuisine. Numerous books already on the shelves (including my own) help identify edible plants in the wild and offer ideas on how to use them. But rarely do their authors consider the possibility of growing edible wild things indoors.

We bring our herbs inside for the winter. We sprout alfalfa and mung beans by the kitchen sink. Why not bring a few common edible wild plants indoors for the year or for a season? Whether you live in the country, with wild things at easy access, or whether you live in the city and take an occasional jaunt to the wild, I think you'll find that the convenience of a wild windowsill garden makes including wild things in your everyday menu all that much more fun.

D A N D E L I O N

(Taraxacum officinale)

Let's start with the dandelion. Everybody knows it. Jagged little leaves form a springtime rosette cluster. Warm weather sees the leaves turn tougher, to support the upcoming flowerstalk that springs from the center. It blooms a sunshine yellow, closing each night, and days later reappearing as a fluffy puffball, scattering seeds to the slightest wind.

Some cuisines hold the dandelion in high esteem for its tender, nutritious greens. Chefs have even developed methods of growing blanched dandelion leaves—leaves grown in dark places, so only a little chlorophyll develops. The result is more tender, sweeter greens.

In the springtime it's easy to go out and gather dandelion leaves in the wild. In summer, while the plant blooms, the leaves tend to taste bitter. But by gathering living plants in the fall and keeping them growing on the windowsill (or in the closet, if you want blanched greens), you can cook with fresh-grown dandelion leaves all winter long.

When you slip your shovel down alongside a dandelion cluster, you will learn that it grows from a single sturdy taproot that sinks straight down unless it has forked in its growing. The plan therefore calls for a tall, deep pot, or a planting tub if you choose to gather more than a single plant. (And you will want to, if you plan to turn to them for more than an occasional green garnish in the winter.)

Prepare the standard wild plant potting soil mix and allow for drainage out the bottom of the pot. Since you're gathering in autumn, you can do it at just about any time of the day; but evening is probably best, to give the plants a rest before they need to respond to the sun again. Set roots straight down into your tub of soil, making sure the juncture of soil and root is tight by watering once you've set in the plants. Settle the plants into the soil at about the same level they had chosen for themselves outdoors. Dandelions hug the ground, so this position will be easy to determine. Clip off any flower starts or damaged leaves.

Dandelions will grow in sun or shade. In the sun, you will need to catch any flowering efforts. Dandelion buds can be eaten, too, as well as the greens, so don't just throw them away. When you harvest the greens, clip from the inside out. The newer the leaf, the more sweet and tender they taste. Leave a healthy outer ring of large leaves to support the plant's continued growing. Keep the soil somewhat moist, but do not overwater. Timing will depend on the tub's material, the consistency of your soil, lighting, and the plant's rate of growth, but always let the soil surface dry out past the wet-to-the-touch stage before you add more water.

Since before the Renaissance, herbalists have valued the dandelion—then more highly than we do now. Its high vitamin A and iron content make it a remarkably nutritious green, considering it's a weed. Citizens of Vineland, New Jersey, know how valuable dandelions are. They brag at living in the "Dandelion Capital of the World." Among their favorite recipes is Dandelions in Marinara Sauce, made by adding chopped dandelion greens to meatless tomato sauce and cooking until the greens are tender. Just before serving, beat into the sauce 1 egg and 1 tablespoon grated Parmesan cheese for each cup of sauce you started with. They suggest it be served over boiled potatoes, but it sounds like a wild spaghetti sauce to me.

If you're industrious, you can gather plants enough to grow dandelions to feed your family all winter. And if you're simply curious, why not try to grow two or three this year? See how easy it is to keep them thriving, and how tasty it is to add fresh dandelion greens to a winter meal.

CHICORY

(Cichorium intybus)

Chicory is known by many for its dried and roasted roots. They are used, primarily in Creole kitchens, to enhance the flavor of coffee. Roasted until they turn a toasty brown and their sugary taste comes through, then ground in with deep-brown coffee beans, chicory root adds special flavor to Louisiana brews.

Others know chicory for its greens, and it's for those greens that one would gather it for indoor growing. Horticulturists have developed strains of chicory that leaf up broad and sweet, but wild chicory leaves grow narrow and somewhat bitter. But proper preparation can make wild chicory greens a delicacy as special as the roots in Creole coffee.

Those who gather chicory in the wild look for it in the springtime, before it begins to blossom. But those who go out looking for chicory plants to pot, particularly if this is their first outing looking for chicory, may find the plant much easier to identify in its full summer bloom.

It lines many roadsides, fills in at the side of fields, its sky-blue flowers opening on an early August morning but closing by the heat of noon.

If you have the opportunity to pinpoint chicory's location, then come back to gather plants a month later, after the bloom, do so. Otherwise, gather chicory plants in blossom, but cut back the flower stalks when you do.

Once you begin digging in around a chicory plant you'll notice how tough its root system is. It grows from a hardy, weedy taproot, and you'll be lucky if your shovel can unearth it unharmed. Locate a chicory stand on the side of a bank or some similar place where the roots are more easily exposed, and it will be an easier gathering. On a roadside you may have to struggle with the hard-packed soil chicory's made to maneuver, and it will be a much more arduous task just to dig up the weed.

If you'd like to set in a little patch of indoor chicory to grow tasty greens for winter salads, then plan to gather at least a dozen chicory roots to take home. Follow the flowering stalk down, and chances are you'll find roots down under in both of their annual cycles: some sprouting tall flowerstalks and some just setting leaves. Choose the leafy plants of this biennial if you have the choice.

Back home, provide your chicory patch with a pot wide and deep enough to give each root a four-inch perimeter of space. For a dozen chicory roots, in other words, you might find a planter two feet long and eight or ten inches wide sufficient. Your pot or planter should be at least eight inches deep, to give those taproots room to spread and support their leafy growing.

Chicory does fine in our wild plant potting soil. It's not that particular about where it grows—in fact, it probably did just fine in the wild under much poorer conditions. Set in the roots at about the same soil depth as they had chosen in their native habitat. If you picked them from a crowded, weedy spot, you may find that their crowns were shaded by greenery, not soil, and you may decide to tip them in a little deeper. Just be sure that you cover the top of the root system well without clogging the growing crown with soil as you sprinkle.

Water the newly potted chicory roots well, being sure your pot provides ample drainage. The first watering secures the contact between sensitive root hairs and soil, but from here on in, take care not to overwater. As you'll see if you look around at chicory in the wild, it does fine in near-drought conditions. Not that we ought to treat a potted weed to the worst possible state it can handle, but those extremes suggest the direction in which a windowsill wild plant gardener should moderate.

The more sunlight you can give your windowsill chicory, the more leaf growth you will foster. The French chefs who hide their chicory in the cellar prefer leaves grown white and tender, blanched like the dandelion. But you sacrifice flavor and nourishment for gourmet tenderness that way. It's nice to know, though, that chicory will sprout even in a little daylight, and that in fact some indoor chicory grows in the dark.

When harvesting your windowsill or cellar garden of chicory, take care not to strip so many of the tasty little leaves that the plants have nothing from which to start over. I made that mistake myself. The leaves were growing six inches tall; I wanted them for a salad. I took a pair of scissors and clip, clip, clip, no more chicory leaf at all. I thought for sure those tough old roots would stand for my denuding. But no—they just turned around and blended right into the soil. If I had left even a single leaf sprouting from each of the roots, I'd still have chicory growing at the window.

P O K E

(Phytolacca americana)

Most country folk in the Southeast love their poke. It's a common spring ritual to go out and gather the young shoots of this prolific plant, before the summer grows hot and the poke grows weedy. Country folk know that they have to find poke before the plant matures and before the poison that always dwells in its perennial taproot is synthesized in its spreading leaves. Another way to assure oneself of bland, sweet, edible, early sprouts of poke is to grow them indoors for windowsill poke salad supreme.

_____

Poke is easier to identify during its autumn fruiting than as it sprouts. Tall stands of massive bending plants line fence rows, roadsides, and yard and garden edges from Maine to Texas. The plants can reach six or seven feet tall. They bloom a white raceme in midsummer, and by August hold long clusters of juicy purple berries. Since the poison occurs in the seeds, children ought to be warned away from the poke. But those luscious berries can be a signal to the gatherer of poke plants to pot indoors—a signal to come back when the weather's turning cold.

The winter freeze turns pokeweed to a skeleton. Hollow, bleached stalks remain, sometimes still hung with berries, but underneath them, underground, still spreads the massive taproot, sometimes six inches across at the crown, sometimes three, four, or more feet deep.

To gather a poke root to plant for indoor sprouting, wait until frost has come. Follow the network of stalks down to their base, and dig in around them. You need not worry about unearthing the entire length of root. Just dig in around the crown, letting the shovel slice the root at a depth of six to eight inches. You'll come up with a big chunk of fibrous material, and you'll probably see on its warty topside the hint of next season's sprouts to come. Each crown will shoot up at least half a dozen sprouts for you before spring sprouts outside, so gather whatever number of poke crowns you wish, according to appetite and space for planting.

Medical literature does report some instances of skin irritation developed through digging up poke root, and experts warn that even more serious internal disturbances might occur if toxins from the poke root entered the bloodstream through a cut or scrape. Gloves and shovels should guard you from directly struggling with the sturdy root of poke.

A large, shallow planting bed will work for poke sprouts, or you can treat those massive roots to larger pots if you wish. The pot you plant your poke in need not be pretty, because you will hide it away. Poke naturally thrives in the toughest of conditions, so you need not provide it with especially rich or fine soil. Give poke roots the standard wild plant potting soil, and you will be treating them to better than what they usually have.

My first poke experiment involved planting the roots horizontally in a wooden wine crate, four inches deep and a foot and a half square. The next year I stuck poke roots vertically into eight-inch plastic pots. Both plans worked well. A metal window box or even a shallow plastic dishpan would work, as long as the container is punctured to give good drainage.

Sprinkle half an inch of soil in the bottom of your sprouting bed, then tip in the pieces of poke root, crown up, just as they grow outside. Cover them over with more soil. You can leave some tip of poke crown showing, but cover most of the root parts with dirt. Water thoroughly, to assure good contact between root and dirt, and set the sprouting bed in a cool, dark place to winter over.

Monthly sprinkles of water, just to assure that the bed doesn't turn bone-dry, are all you'll have to give your poke plants over winter. They will enjoy the same quiet dormancy as their neighboring plants outdoors, but without the hardships of snow and freezing, the heavings of freeze gone to thaw.

When the first signs of spring emerge in the landscape outdoors, you'll want to start watching your poke bed more closely. Who knows what prompts it to happen, but sure enough, one day you'll look to see the fat little fingers of poke sprouting green. When you see that beginning, become more vigilant in watering. You may wish to set the poke bed out in the light now, but it still doesn't need the direct light of a sunny window. In fact, poke sprouts grown, say, under a desk or table—in the diffuse light of a room, yet not on the windowsill—sprout white, sweet, somewhat blanched, and taste more delicate than the poke sprouting outdoors one month later.

I'd say the indoor poke crop is ready for picking once the sprouts reach four to six inches tall. In the wild, people gather them even taller, but the special pleasure of tender forced poke requires early picking. Besides, any poke picker who knows what she's doing picks the smallest sprouts outdoors as well.

How to use your homegrown poke? The classic recipe says to boil and boil, but the tenderness of poke grown indoors does not require so much cooking. Indoor-grown poke sprouts only need a quick steaming.

If you grow only a single root's worth of poke, you can serve it for some special dinnertime, some night when you feel like celebrating the oncoming spring. If you plant a thicker batch of poke, it can become a more regular feature of your early-spring cuisine, or you can blend it into some concoction like my favorite, Poke Pie.

Begin with 2 to 4 cups of freshly picked poke sprouts. Give them a brief steaming. In a casserole dish suited for both stovetop and oven use, sauté 1 onion, 2 garlic cloves, a smattering of herbs like basil and rosemary, and ¼ teaspoon of salt in 2 tablespoons olive oil or butter. Once the onions are tender, turn off the heat and stir in the steamed sprouts. Sprinkle over the vegetables 1 cup of cornmeal. Now beat 2 eggs, pour them over, and mix the whole mess up. Sprinkle a little grated Parmesan cheese on top and bake at 350 degrees for 30 minutes.

Your poke bed may try to keep up pace with your picking, but I think you'll find that each new generation of sprouts is a little weaker, a little thinner than the last, until it's time to chuck out the old roots and declare that spring has begun. You will need more than a windowsill to foster full-grown poke plants indoors, so you may decide that it's better to gather more poke roots from the wild next autumn for an early taste of spring next year.

O X A L I S

(Oxalis spp.)

Oxalis, a weed just as familiar in backyards and gardens as it is on the forest floor, grows its trefoil of heart-shaped leaves once the weather warms. At least eight hundred distinct species of oxalis grow worldwide, and there are more than twenty in our United States and Canada. Among those species are several tropical varieties often grown as house-plants, like *Oxalis regnelli,* among many others. While many of our native wild oxalis plants are smaller in leaf and flower than the oxalis gathered from tropical climes, our wild natives can be adopted and will do quite well on a windowsill.

The yellow wood sorrel, best known east and west as a yard and garden weed, makes a good example of the promise of oxalis as a house-plant. It's known by many common names—sourgrass, trefoil, pickle-weed, shamrock. Many people mistakenly call it clover, just because of its three-leaf shape. And many people recognize it as a plant they nibbled on in childhood—a plant forgotten, once adult habits turned their eyes from wild plants underfoot.

Yellow wood sorrel branches from a single stalk supported by a little fibrous network of roots. Some oxalis species grow from a tuber, making them easier to gather and easier to pot. The trick with a yellow wood sorrel is to gather at a time of day that will not be stressful to the plant, to gather a plant that's proved itself hardy already, and to dig up a clump of supporting soil when you dig up the wildflower root system, to form a cushion while you carry it home.

From the fibrous root system stand one or more straight little stalks, off of which branch leaves and flowers. By warm weather, from the same node that sends out a leafy stalk, a pretty little five-petaled yellow flower opens. Once pollinated, the seedpod develops: a long, thin pod, star-shaped in cross section, containing numerous little wood sorrel seeds for future sprouting. Every part of this little plant—leaf, flower, and seed-pod—carries the characteristic tangy acidic flavor that kids love and adults can enjoy as well.

For good-looking houseplants in a kitchen window, you may find that you need to sink the stalk of oxalis down under the soil surface deeper than the plant stood on its own. This method of transplanting will encourage a bushy appearance, rather than the wild, lanky look of a skinny outside oxalis reaching over neighboring grasses to get some sun. For the very same reason, you may prefer to pot up four or five oxalis plants together in a larger pot, rather than putting a single plant into a smaller one. Tip the central stalk outward from the center just slightly, fan the plants around the outer edge of the pot, and you'll have a full, luxurious pot of soon-to-bloom oxalis.

Yellow oxalis blooms sunny yellow; a mountain oxalis blooms white or pink; redwood oxalis blooms in lavender. Their flowers are not showy, but predictable and numerous. Clip any flowers off an oxalis plant when you gather it to pot it, and you'll be assured of a longer bloom once the plant gets used to your house. Indeed, I've found that a win-dowsill oxalis, probably because it faces stress, tends to bloom more heavily than those left behind. So I try to keep oxalis flowers clipped; I enjoy them, then I pinch them, forbidding them to set seed. For once the plant goes seedy, the leaves disappear and it dwindles and dies.

Oxalis likes a well-drained soil, and it seeks out high acidity. You can increase the acidity of your wild plant potting soil by occasionally watering your windowsill oxalis with the last of a pot of black tea.

Oxalis would prefer the gentle diffuse light of an eastern or western window, although a southern exposure might bring on more blooms. But the more light you give it, the more watering it will need. Oxalis seems to like a lot of water.

Your oxalis plant won't get up and walk around, but it will exhibit movement. Plants are living, and they move too, even without a wind blowing through them. Botanists call their daily cycles of movement "circadian rhythms" and are still seeking explanations of how a plant's inner clockworks operate. You'll probably notice that your wild oxalis calibrates itself to the seasons outside, no matter what lighting you do or don't give it from within. I take this pattern as just another reminder that even though I can bring wild things into my kitchen, they remain linked with the world outside.

That pleasant acidic zing of oxalis can be useful in your cuisine. Try sprinkling just a few clipped trefoil leaves over a salad, or use their lovely shapes and subtle flavor to garnish a serving platter with vegetables or fish. They have a pleasing shape, a mild little crunch, and that sweet tangy flavor.

But oxalis leaves and seedpods should be considered only a garnish, not a staple green. High in oxalic acid, an organic compound actually named after these plants, oxalis could be harmful if ingested in large quantities. The damage can occur over time, because too much oxalic acid collects in the kidney, binding with calcium in the body, creating crystals of calcium oxalate. Not only do these crystals obstruct proper organ functioning, but since their production ties up otherwise useful calcium, they also actually deplete the body of that important mineral.

This warning should be taken as a serious guideline for moderation, but occasional indulgence in a wood sorrel leaf here and there will not cause harm. I'll pass the facts along to you, and let you decide for yourself whether you wish to grow oxalis to ornament your menu or just your windowsill.

PURSLANE

(Portulaca oleracea)

Purslane needs a hot sun to sprout its flat, oval, succulent leaves and open its diminutive yellow flowers. It grows coast to coast, wherever it finds an area clear enough that it can spread out flat and sassy. Most gardeners curse the purslane, because garden plots are just the kind of place it likes to take over. But consider the purslane as a plant to gather and pot, and you might just have to reconsider your opinion of it.

Today purslane is counted a weed, but it was sown and harvested in colonial kitchen gardens. Originally a plant native to India, it made its way through Europe and then, in the seed pouches of colonists traveling west, on to America, where now it scatters cities and farmsteads alike. But rarely does anyone consider purslane a valuable plant anymore. Just a weed.

But taste a leaf or tender stalk of purslane, and you may begin to change your mind. Related to the garden flower moss rose, it has those same smooth round shiny stalks, but the leaves of the edible purslane grow flat and oval, succulent and crisp. The longer the growing season, the thicker the stalk and the larger a plant purslane will grow. Its flowers are tiny and nondescript, quickly maturing into two-part seedpods that soon pop open and spill out tiny black purslane seeds.

Gathering seed of purslane isn't too hard. You can pull up a whole plant as it flowers or clip off a productive branch, then spread it out on a newspaper to dry. As the leaves shrivel, the seedpods mature. In a week, the plant will have dwindled to nothing but a few dry stalks. Give it a shake, though, and out will tumble hundreds of minuscule black seeds. They do quite well for edible sprouts (discussed later in this chapter), or you can sprout your own indoor purslane plants.

But if you've found a healthy purslane—and particularly if you're doing some gardener friend a favor by digging it out—you can also get your pot of purslane started by transplanting from the wild.

Purslane seems quite indiscriminate about the kind of soil it needs. Our wild plant potting soil mix suits it well—it's higher quality than the purslane often chooses for itself. But I figure, might as well pamper the purslane. Purslane does not need a lot of water—it's accustomed to desert spots—but adequate watering is important, particularly as you're establishing the plant within its new potted home.

The roots don't grow too deep and don't spread too far, so you'll have to take some care in transplanting, by troweling in around the base of the purslane, to get soil encompassing the roots. Sometimes purslane plants spill all over the ground, so one must trace their network of stalks back to the single point at which they've rooted. Don't just yank it out, because you'll leave precious roots behind. Settle the rooted plant into your potting soil and bank some soil up over the level at which the plant met dirt in the wild.

Purslane will prefer a sunny spot in your window—in fact, give it the most sunlight you can. But watch out for leaf burn in a sunny location. Avoid watering it in the heat of the day. If the leaves lose luster, rescue it by placing it in a shadier spot for a while. Adequate light will bring out the little yellow purslane bloom, which in the wild soon unfolds into a capped seedpod full of many tiny seeds. If you catch them, snip the flowers, to keep the plant from going to seed. The longer you can keep it greening, the longer you can enjoy it on your windowsill.

You will probably use purslane primarily as a green garnish—not, however, as with the oxalis, because of any harmful components in the plant. Purslane is quite healthy and safe, and has been eaten by humans for centuries. But if you begin to count on your plant of purslane for more than just a garnish, pretty soon you will have plucked the windowsill purslane back to the nub, and you'll have to sprout more purslane for the summer kitchen garden.

C H I C K W E E D

(Stellaria media)

Once the purslane's season gets the better of you, setting seed and dying back no matter how you tend it, it's time to look around the fields and garden for a fall wildflower to bring onto the kitchen sill. Now try chickweed, a valuable windowsill weed because it will keep growing all winter.

Several wild members of the Pink family are known as chickweed. The one I've grown on my windowsill is *Stellaria media*, common chickweed, its botanical name reflecting its starry white flowers. A common garden weed, it's often thrown away in disgust by overzealous gardeners. I've made a habit of encouraging people to taste the chickweed before they curse it. Totally edible, chickweed's really quite delicious. It grows in the cooler seasons, sprouting out in October or November, basking in whatever winter sunshine it might find, returning full force come March or April. It flowers minute white starlets in midspring, and by summer it has succumbed to the heat. Chickweed bows out while tougher summer weeds take over, then it comes back into view once they've passed their prime.

Now I have another rave review for chickweed. You can grow it, quite easily, in windowsill pots all winter long. It maintains its bushiness and its healthy green color, given your help. And those vitamins and minerals that so many weeds offer are right there at your fingertips, on your windowsill.

In fact, chickweed was one of the plants that got me started in this adventure of growing wildflowers on the windowsill. Once or twice I gathered chickweed plants or seeds quite by accident, in a bucket of soil I brought inside for other purposes. I watched that chickweed grow. It got good and bushy and didn't need a lot of care, and the idea soon got planted: Why not grow a chickweed plant on purpose?

Keep your eyes open, as the autumn days grow shorter, for sprouting chickweed in among the fallen leaves. It's a lighter green than many, and grows with small oval leaves opposite one another on a slender, fibrous stalk.

Chickweed has one curious identifying feature by which you can single it out from all other weeds it might resemble. Running along each stalk, node to node, can be found a thin, single line of hairs. Take a look. It's not what you'd call a hairy stalk—a single line of hairs, usually at a different place between each pair of nodes, characterizes the chickweed.

Dig in under a bunch of chickweed, and you'll usually find a complicated network of fibrous roots. Sometimes one root system bears many stalks, and sometimes many plants cluster together. Whichever, you can easily dig up a good healthy cluster of chickweed to pot in a medium- to large-size pot. The pot needn't be too deep. I've found that often if I dig up a well-grown clump of chickweed and plunk it into a pot, quite a bit of greenery will die back, making it look as if the chickweed's dying. But somehow the root system soaks up the water I provide it, and in a week, after shedding a few stray tendrils, it's back to growing green and strong.

Chickweed has a lovely way of draping over the edge of pots, offering the beauty of a nursery plant like baby tears or wandering Jew. And if you keep picking it, it just grows more. Its woodland cousin great chickweed (*Stellaria pubera*) will grow larger leaves and flowers. It prefers more private, shady environments, deeper woods and forests, than the doorsteps common chickweed chooses. But it should take to pots well too.

Since you gather chickweed for wintertime growing, it really doesn't matter which window you place it in. It does okay in natural shade, so it will do okay in a western or northern exposure. Your southern and eastern windows, in midwinter, will not over-sun it either. Keep it well watered, not soggy, and watch it begin to grow.

How to use your chickweed? First, take a nibble. It's fresh like lettuce, fibrous like cabbage, real bunny food. If you've brought in a large potful, you can gather portions big enough to mingle in with other salad greens. If you've just filled a little pot with sprigs of chickweed, you can still clip them off and use them as you would parsley, as a lovely garnish of green. Be sure to encourage your guests to eat their weeds.

Chickweed likes to be kept trim and tidy. The more you clip it, the more it will keep on growing and give you more greens. But the time will come when your chickweed, following the urge of nature, will start to flower. Keep clipping—you should be able to get another month's use out of the plant before the heat and day length force it to become tough and gawky. Then it's time to compost it, plant, dirt, and all, until next autumn, when you can gather fresh chickweed for wintertime again.

WILD ONIONS

(*Allium* spp.)

Dozens of wild onion species grow across this continent, and there is no way I could test the indoor growing of them all. But my guess is that most of these *Allium* species are hardy enough to take the move. Many

will not flower as they might in the wild. But all will offer odoriferous greenery, an interesting gathering to tide your winter windowsill over into the spring.

The wild onion I know best goes by the local name onion grass, probably because people know it best by its fragrance in the air during summer mowing. Technically, this plant is a wild garlic. You can tell by the tiny cloves that cleave to a central underground bulb. Those cloves drive farmers and gardeners mad by staying in the soil even after a thorough weeding. But the same prodigious growth patterns that make wild garlic a garden pest make it a fail-safe wild green for the windowsill.

The blue-green leaves of the wild garlic sprout through melting patches of snow, and that's the time I've found gathering plants of wild garlic most satisfying. Dig one of those clumps up, and you will see the cluster of bulbs and clinging cloves out of which it's sprouting. Set that cluster into agreeable wild plant potting soil, and it will keep its chivy growth going on into warmer weather.

It's best to trim back the potted wild garlic. Use it like chives sprinkled over salads, sauces, soups, and eggs. Cut it back drastically, if you want to—those bulbs down under have enough go-power to sprout new tender greens, more tasty than the old, tough ones. Left untrimmed, my wild garlic plants curl under. They like a constant pruning. It keeps them growing green and lively until the wood sorrel sprouts out and the seasonal cycle of a wild windowsill garden begins again.

WATERCRESS

(Nasturtium officinale)

Of course, watercress prefers the bracing environment of a bubbling mountain stream. But you can grow it indoors if you work at it. Find a wild patch of watercress, dislodge a few sprigs, and you'll see the simple and straightforward way that it grows. From nodes lower down on the stalk sprout the hairy, waterbound roots; from nodes higher up sprout the fibrous, green, sun-seeking leaves. Rarely is a watercress plant so tightly fastened in its woodland streambed that it resists a gentle tug. Maintain some roots, keep them moist on the way home, and you can get watercress started at home for green garnishes and salads.

The vascular system of a plant that grows in water develops differently from that of an earth-dwelling plant. Whereas in a soil-loving weed the xylem channels are tightly enmeshed with supportive tissue, in a water-dweller they are larger, taking up more of the entire root and stem structure, since the water running through them actually offers the plant some support. So you must provide a water-dwelling plant like watercress with a fairly moist environment, in a medium that holds water as well as the roots. You can't create a stream bed on your windowsill, but you can recreate the essential conditions so that watercress will survive quite happily in an indoor home.

I gathered watercress plants from a friend's bubbling spring on New Year's Day. By chance, the same friend foisted on me that day a miniature barbecue grill, a foot in diameter, three inches deep, with detachable legs that stood the pan up about six inches. I didn't really want the barbecue—seemed like a cheap piece of junk to me. But Kathy insisted, jokingly, and I went ahead and took it. Took it, along with the sprigs of watercress I found in the chilly spring.

Only when I got home and set about potting up the watercress did I realize that that barbecue rig was no useless piece of junk—it was a perfect watercress planter.

I lined the circular pan with newspapers, then filled it to within half an inch of the rim with a mixture of perlite and vermiculite—three parts perlite to one part vermiculite, a soil mixture designed to hold plenty of water rather than nourish the plants. I watered down the medium, then gently pushed into it rooted sprigs of watercress and tossed perlite back over the roots so none were exposed. In the center of the pan, just for fun, I placed another variety of wild cress—*Cardamine hirsuta*—found growing as a winter green on the spring bank. It's one of the first wild blooms in our neck of the woods, with delicate little white flowers that can open as early as January.

Then I watered the pan of watercress once more, so thoroughly that water drained out abundantly through the holes in the side of the barbecue made for the legs to slip through. I placed it about a foot below my grow-light setup, and sat back to watch it grow.

The perlite absorbs so much moisture that days can go by without my watering the watercress, and it still feels damp. But I try to remember to give it a splash at least every third day. Although the plant is designed to sit in water, letting it sit in well-moistened perlite is a good second best. The sprigs that might spread horizontally are stretching up, perhaps a bit thinner than if they were in the full sun, winter sun though it might be. The indoor leaves grow a bit smaller. But they certainly are full of that pungent hot flavor of watercress, whether they grow outdoors or in.

The weather that year turned wretched just after New Year's, snow and ice everywhere. So I enjoyed a special treat, considering that the spring pool from which I borrowed those leafy greens was icy, so nothing could be gathered from it. From my little barbecue pit full of perlite, I could snip watercress for sandwiches and salads, no matter how icy it was outside.

WILD SPROUTS

(Chenopodium album and other spp.)

Sprouts have shed their counterculture reputation. You will be served alfalfa or mung sprouts at a gourmet luncheon just as frequently as you'll see them in health-food or vegetarian eateries these days. They're tasty, crunchy, and healthful. They lend life to sandwiches and salads. They aren't that hard to grow in one's own kitchen, and the seeds from which to start them are getting easier and easier to find.

With all this increased familiarity with sprouts on the menu, it shouldn't come as a surprise that some of us who gather wild things have begun to experiment with sprouting wild things too. Anyone who's watched an unplowed patch of garden in springtime knows in what abundance many common weed seeds sprout. And anyone who has in-

quired into the nutritional content of edible weeds knows that they rival, often exceed, their cultivated cousins. Stands to reason that weed seeds would make good sprouts: easy to come by, not that hard to sprout, and highly nutritious too.

By now I've tested several different sorts of weed seeds to discover their usefulness in the kitchen as sprouts. I've come up with some successes too. My favorites to date include lamb's quarters and dandelion. Failures include plantain and burdock seed. Combining my results with those of fellow gatherer Bill Chapman, who's been sprouting wild seeds for years now, I think I can offer some general rules of thumb and provisos regarding the possibilities in wild sprouts.

Sprouting wild seeds involves numerous activities beyond the simple attempt to get the seeds to start growing. Wild sproutable seeds don't come cleaned and packaged. You have to identify and gather them from the wild. The most promising plants that grow seeds appropriate for sprouting are some of the most common weeds around. Dandelions don't need discussion. Lamb's quarters (also called goosefoot, pigweed, or wild spinach) should be familiar to most hunters of edible wild plants. Its shield-shaped leaves show a silvery sheen. It can grow to four or five feet tall, preferring the nitrogen-rich soil of gardens, compost piles, and dumps. It's a ubiquitous weed.

Once identified, these two plants present two quite different tasks to the person set upon collecting their seed. Dandelion seed heads puff up tender and familiar: those white, fluffy, blowaway spheres of winged seeds. Take a look at a dandelion gone to seed, and you'll see how, upon a white pincushion, dozens of quarter-inch-long slender seeds cluster, each topped with a feathery whirl of fluff. Every schoolchild knows why. Give a puff, and the constellation of dandelion seeds disperses, each seed scattering, floating gently on the wind. If you want to sprout them at home, you have to catch them early.

I've found that the easiest way to capture ripe dandelion seeds, which don't even show themselves until they're ready to fly, is to enclose the entire puffball in a paper envelope. Gather the whole thing, wings and all. By flattening the sphere in your pocket as you carry it home, you're already separating seeds from wings.

Lamb's quarters seed heads present quite a different challenge. As the summer nears its end, these plants develop gnarled little flowering clusters out along their branch ends. Without any petals to show one the way, it's often hard to tell when lamb's quarters is flowering from when it's holding a ripe stock of seed. The best way is to crumble a flowerstalk between your fingers; if, from out of that handful of growing green, shiny little black seeds the size of pinheads fall free, you know it's time to gather seed of lamb's quarters.

A single plant of lamb's quarters might produce almost a pound of seed, since it branches many times and at the tip of each branch it holds many seeds. The branches can simply be clipped below the seed-bearing cluster and hung upside down in a grocery bag to dry. Or, instead, seed heads can be shattered over a bag or envelope, resulting in a bumpy mixture of lamb's quarters seed and chaff. Store these gatherings in a dry, dark place for a month, and the next stage of sprouting weed seeds will be made much easier.

No matter which plant you gather seeds from, your next task is separating those seeds from the chaff, or all that extra plant material—the remaining flower parts, the stalks and husks and wings that carry a seed through to maturity but play no part in seeing it sprout. Now comes the process in which one recognizes the great advantages of industrial food processing; now comes the state when one must remember, if one can, pictures of American Indian women thrashing grain in large woven baskets, tossing it into the wind, seeing the chaff fly away, watching the seeds settle and stay.

The underlying principle of winnowing by hand arises from the fact that all those bits of dried chaff weigh considerably less than the seeds that they surround. You don't need a fancy basket to thrash a few weed seeds. Tip out a quarter to half a cup of seed material onto a dinner plate or large, shallow soup bowl. With your fingers, coax apart as best you can any plant material still clinging to the seeds. Already you begin to see how the seeds run together when you tip the plate up. Use your wind-power or a very gentle electric fan, and you can set the chaff flying without disturbing that collection of seed. Turn the plate and reposition, just like a miner sifting through stream pebbles and silt for gold.

We're used to perfectly cleaned seeds for sprouting. At the grocery, alfalfa and mung beans come chaff-free. But you need not set such high standards for your own home effort at cleaning sproutable weed seeds. The bit of leftover chaff won't hinder the process of sprouting. It will float on the surface of the water as you soak your seeds, and you can toss it off as you begin to sprout them.

Weed seeds sprout by the same easy methods followed for any other home-sprouted seeds. Considering their relatively small size, I've usually sprouted weed seeds in a half-pint jelly jar, covered over with a swatch of fine cheesecloth, held in place with a jar ring or a rubber band. I start with at least a tablespoon of cleaned weed seed, because these sprouts don't grow to be that big. I place the seed in the jar and fill it with water overnight. This soaking stage loosens up the tough, protective seed coat and starts the cycle of newborn growth deep within the seed.

The next morning I tip off all excess water and set the jar top down in a saucer or sieve. One of the most useful stands I've found for this purpose is in fact a plastic sprouting lid, made to fit a wide-mouth quart jar, therefore large enough to cradle the little half-pints I use. Whatever you use, it should be something that allows air circulation in and drainage out of the jar in which the seeds sit sprouting.

Twice a day I rinse the sprouts in cool water, setting the jar again on end. Speed of sprouting depends on the temperature of the environment in which you've set your seeds. Since sprouts seem a perfect wintertime food—fresh, homegrown greens when no others can be found—they will take at least a week to show noticeable sprouting. Weed seeds don't pop open as quickly as some of the cultivars now grown especially for sprouting. But keep faith and stay regular in your rinsing. The seeds should always have a little moisture surrounding them.

Weed seeds will take longer to sprout, and they'll sprout smaller than many we're accustomed to in our kitchens. After two and a half weeks, both dandelion and lamb's quarters seeds will produce a tumbled tangle of seeds. Most of what you first see shooting from a kitchen sprout is the radicle or emerging rootlet of the plant. Leave it growing a little bit longer and you begin to see the plumule or emerging green growth too. Sprouts grown in a sunny location tend more to leaf out, taking on a greener color and, in the case of lamb's quarters, a characteristic shade of red. Slow-growing as they are, a crop of weed sprouts can provide salad or sandwich garnishes over several days. Pinch a meal's worth from the jar, but keep the rest rinsed and growing.

British kitchens grow sprouts a different way, and it's a method one might follow well with weed seeds. Instead of sprouting seeds in air, they give them a moisture-retentive growing medium like perlite or vermiculite. They scatter seeds onto a well-watered shallow flat. The chaff just blends in with the growing medium. They let them grow in a moderately sunny location, then clip them off at the stalk, leaving the rootlets behind and serving green sprouts only. This method requires a longer growing period, since one waits for the cotyledons or initial pair of leafy greens to unfold completely. But it's a convenient and pleasing way to keep a garden of weed sprouts popping up on a kitchen windowsill.

Doubtless many other weeds sprout green and tender. Bill Chapman higly favors the seeds of wild mustards like peppergrass or wintercress. He also recommends the sprouts of wild salsify, a magnificent wild thing most likely to catch your eye the day it opens its fluffy round seed head, shaped like a dandelion seed head, five inches wide. Salsify seeds grow to well over half an inch long, and Bill says that of all the wild seeds he's sprouted, wild salsify grows the biggest, crunchiest sprouts of all.

Sprouting wild things isn't easy. It takes more work than buying seeds or sprouts at the store. You must be ready to identify a plant and its seeds as edible, to gather and dry the harvest, to thrash the seed from chaff, and to endure a week or more of patient waiting until you see signs of life. But the procedure offers more than one reward. Not only do you get to taste the new crunch of weed sprouts with your meal but you also enrich your own life with the flavor of life long ago, when harvest and thrashing played a necessary part in the cycles of gathering food for life.

CHAPTER 4

Wild Herbs on the Windowsill

Even if you stocked your wild windowsill garden with every edible wild thing you could grow, you still couldn't cultivate your family's vegetable needs for over the winter. I'll admit it. A windowsill wild garden offers varieties of greens, greens different from those available at the grocery store, in sampling, not staple, quantities. Given these limits, growing wild herbs on the windowsill might seem a more appropriate occupation. Grow a single herb plant and you provide a year's supply of pinches for seasonings and teas.

The word *herb* literally means a deciduous nonwoody plant, so technically almost every weed we see falls into this category. But to most people's sensibilities, the word *herb* singles out those plants high in flavor, fragrance, or medicinal properties. Their potency dwells in volatile oils and in chemical compounds like alkaloids and glycosides. Their usefulness arises when those oils and compounds mingle with foods as we cook them or with hot water as we brew tea. Just a bit of a flavorful herb makes a favorite dish lean toward green; just a bit of a medicinal herb often soothes the body, bringing out the powers of nature hidden within.

Many herb gardeners have already discovered that outdoor herb plants do splendidly inside. Either they bring herbs in from the garden for winter or they grow them on a city windowsill all year long. Most cooking herbs grow slowly and without great demands for fertilizer, soil constitution, or watering, so they can be adopted easily. Many of them

have wild counterparts that grow well on the windowsill and add wild
flavor, too. So why not, alongside your sage and parsley, set a few wild
herbs growing inside, too?

WILD MINTS

(Labiatae family)

Basil, sage, oregano, thyme—these are some of the old standbys that
people will name when asked about their favorite herbs. These and many
other of our favorite cooking herbs all belong to the Labiatae family—in
other words, they are mints. They have many relatives living in the wild,
which are just as easily propagated in a kitchen setting as their cultivated
cousins. Dozens of species of wild mints grow from coast to coast, in
almost every kind of growing condition. Some grew native to America
from the start, while many were among the favorite plants brought to
this continent by European settlers. Some are more sensitive than others
to their growing terrain; some need lots of sun and grow to be three feet

tall, making them unlikely windowsill companions. But others don't mind shady spots and hug the soil they grow in. Those humbler mints, more than the others, do well indoors on the windowsill.

Among the Labiatae family, both annuals and perennials grow. Either type of mint can be grown indoors, but each is gathered differently. Annual mints are most easily gathered by seed, while perennial mints maintain themselves best when gathered by root or shoot cuttings. If you wish to experiment with mints not mentioned specifically here, begin by determining the plant's growing cycle and take it from there.

Peppermint is a perennial mint whose flavor everyone knows, though more often from candy or chewing gum than from its leafy green. It may be a little harder to find than some of the other wild mints. Old homesteads are often the most likely location. I always hope I've found a bright patch of peppermint in my wanderings, and nine times out of ten I'm disappointed to find some nondescript spearmint instead.

Spearmint's many variations baffle botanists with the urge to classify. Spearmint, horsemint, curled mint, apple mint—all are variations on the theme. It even seems that more than one kind of plant gets called spearmint. The problem arises because these mints cross-pollinate, creating more varieties than botanists care to classify. But they all seem to prefer partial shade and moist dwellings, propagating voluminously and covering the ground. Spearmint is often found near abandoned back stoops or house sites. Years back, cooks recognized the flavorful value of these mints and kept them growing right near the kitchen—if not in it.

Unearth a spearmint plant and you will find a runner underground, thinly covered with bark and no bigger than the plant's own stem. From nodes along that runner shoot new underground branches, covered like the main root with filaments that cling to earth and seek out water. The tip of each branching section terminates in a tender, probing, growing end which eventually wants to shoot aboveground and end up a stalk on its own.

Even a two- or three-inch length of that underground runner, if gathered from the soil and kept moist until you're home, will soon start up a little spearmint sprig of its own. Follow a leafy stalk down underground, then dig in with a trowel, making an eight- to twelve-inch circle around the earthbound roots. Chances are you'll come up with an intricate, intertwined root system—spearmint sprouts, in tones of purple, crisscrossing and trying to grow.

Spearmint usually spreads so wildly that digging up a patch like this actually increases the crop you leave behind. Last summer I gladly agreed to friends coming over and uprooting buckets full of spearmint from our garden edge. They wanted to pot it up for centerpieces for a large June luncheon, plants enough for twenty tables. I was happy to see my spearmint crop diminish. But this year—oh! the spearmint. They say that chamomile likes to be stepped upon. I say that spearmint likes to be gathered. What's left behind seems all the more abundant.

Spearmint is not too particular about soil, and it will do fine set into the standard wild plant potting soil mixture. Allow at least eight inches of pot depth for spearmint. While it seems to grow shallow roots, it will send up tall spikes. The deeper its roots grow, the more stalk they can handle. Tip the roots into your pots a little deeper than the depth they have chosen on their own.

The more sun you can give spearmint, the healthier it will grow. Water in balance with the light you give it. If you must set it in a spot with moderate lighting, water it less frequently. If you can bathe it in a southern exposure (or better yet, on a porch or balcony), it may need watering every other day or so. Even though spearmint inclines toward moist locations in the wild, overwatering can cause rot and fungus to develop.

Spearmint rootstock can be gathered at just about any time of year. As usual, flowering time is not the wisest time to gather, but often hardy spearmint will live through transplantation even then. To assure continued foliage if you gather it in flower, however, clip the stalks as you dig them, leaving only four to six inches of leaf-bearing stalk on the plants you pot. The clipped stalks can be dried for tea or seasoning. Soon enough the rootstock you planted will begin to sprout greenery anew, and fragrant mints will grace your kitchen sill all winter long.

The same principles apply for gathering many other wild perennial mints. Take bergamot, for instance (*Monarda fistulosa*). Unless you've learned the look of that arrow-pointed leaf with its red vein running up the middle, you'll probably not notice bergamot in the wild until it blooms its fragrant midsummer flower. Then you and the bees know it's there. Follow the tall leafstalk down to the roots below. They're probably just as jumbled as a spearmint root system. Dig under eight to ten inches and come up with a handful of dirt and roots. Again, clip off the flowerstalk. It won't survive the journey home, or if it does, it won't maintain itself indoors much longer. Instead, make way for new leaf growth from the perennial roots.

Any taller perennial mint, particularly those with large, heavy flowers, won't bloom for you on the windowsill. They need light more than indoor environments can give them. But their leaves will unfold and thrive, and it's the leaf that holds the minty fragrance. Establish a perennial mint on your windowsill, and even if it doesn't bloom it offers cheerful smells, just for a pinch. Clip a few leaves to flavor a pot of tea or spice up a mint julep. Homesteaders always had some use for the mints at their back-door stoop. Surely you can find many ways to use the mints on your windowsill.

Many people have encountered catnip only in factory-made stuffed mousies—but catnip's a mint that grows wild too, an annual that takes to sprouting or potting. Its leaves are a very light blue-green, heart-shaped overall but evenly scalloped along their edges. The stem, like the stems of all other mints, is decidedly square in shape. Catnip grows in the wildest places, but it has also escaped into alleys and open lots in towns across the continent. It smells a bit mustier than most other mints. It gets stronger as it dries, and has the old-time reputation of putting children to sleep and cats into ecstasy.

While spearmint grows by runners, each stalk standing an inch from the next, catnip grows in bunches. New shoots appear, clustered around the old, and it's not very difficult to separate several stalks off a large plant with a shovel, cutting straight down through stems and leaves into the root system, and coming away with a new catnip plant. Catnip propagates easily by cuttings, too. A single plant from the wild might yield a number of little catnips. Clip stalks arising from down near the ground. Make a clean cut just below a stem node, leaving at least four nodes on the stalk you cut. Carry the cuttings home quickly and carefully, wrapped in damp cloth or paper towel if you'll be out very long.

Back home, you can root those cuttings in water or in soil. While water seems the easier route, the subsequent transfer from water to soil can be difficult; so in the long run, rooting them in soil from the first works the best. For rooting, prepare a medium very high in porous material. A combination of one part wild plant potting soil to two parts perlite will do the job. Treat trimmed cuttings with Rootone, if you wish. Be sure that at least two stem nodes, preferably three, stick well under the rooting medium and keep the soil moist but not waterlogged. Some people create a mini-greenhouse for cuttings by enclosing the pot and plant in a plastic bag, using dowels to keep the plastic from touching the plant and sealing it off with a rubber band around the pot's rim. This plan keeps moisture levels high for the plant, but sometimes tends to promote mold or rotting. If you choose to use a plastic bag, keep an eye on your plants day by day.

You'll know the catnip has grown roots when a gentle tug on the stem no longer pulls the plant out of the soil. If it pulls back, it wants to stay there. It has found a home, thanks to you. At this point, you will do well to transfer the plant to a pot with soil more to its liking: back to the standard wild plant potting soil mixture, since the high perlite concentration guarantees moisture but not nutrients.

Wild catnip seeds can be gathered for sprouting, too, a method that allows you to bring wild plants home without removing them from the wild. By late summer, a healthy catnip plant is blooming its tight little clusters of white-green flowers. By mid-autumn it has set its seed. Double-check to see whether seeds are ripe by rubbing a catnip flower head. If small black seeds tumble into your hands, then the seeds have matured and are ready for picking. Go ahead and clip off several entire catnip flower heads. It's easier to carry them home that way.

The difficulties in thrashing wild seed and methods for doing it are outlined in the previous chapter, in the section on wild sprouts. Thrashing seed to sow is less exacting a task than thrashing wild seed to sprout, since the chaff will simply blend in with the soil in which you start your seed. Don't forgo thrashing altogether, however. You will want to see the seed closely enough to be sure that you don't overload one section of the pot you plant in while depriving the other section of seeds altogether. Catnip seed, while small, is relatively manageable. Twenty to forty seeds will amply sow a four-inch pot, allowing for the low germination rate to be expected from seeds gathered from the wild and sprouted in unusual conditions.

Sprout annual mints like catnip in a pot full of wild plant potting soil. Thoroughly moisten the soil before the seeds ever reach it. See that water flows throughout the soil and out the hole at the bottom of the pot. Then sprinkle the seed uniformly over the surface of the soil. Touch them under gently with a toothpick or the cap of a pen or any other instrument that will set them just under the soil without creating a gully above them. The rule of thumb for how deep a seed sits under the soil is no deeper than twice its own dimension. Considering that catnip seeds are little specks of black, they need not dive very deep beneath the surface of the soil in which you sprout them. Keep the soil moist, not wet. Keep it out of the sun until you see a hint of green arising. Then set it in a sunny space, being careful to gauge water needs accordingly. The less sun you give it, the more that blue-green color in its leaves shines through. Fertilize the growing plant monthly, and be sure not to show your cat where you put the catnip.

Another member of the mint family easily sprouted from seed is motherwort (*Leonurus cardiaca*). Unlike the other mints already mentioned, this one has no minty scent. But it's a handsome plant, with broad, frequent leaves. It grows up to two and a half feet tall in nature, but you can keep it trimmed back to a pleasant eight to ten inches at home. In late summer, go out looking along country roads and field edges for the prickly seed-bearing flower heads of this unusual mint. Bring home a stalk, hang it upside down in a paper bag to dry, and within a week or two (depending on the weather) you can separate from the pin-sharp seed clusters those little black seeds filled with the promise of more plants to bear. Sow just as you would the seed of catnip, offering as much sun as possible once the green leaves sprout, and you can get to know this less familiar member of the mint family in your own home.

You wouldn't want to sprinkle herb of motherwort in your soup or salad dressing. It's a very bitter mint indeed. Its suggestive name points to the one medicinal purpose for which this wild plant has been used: as a soothing bitter tea during cramp-ridden menstrual periods. Despite the fact that I've grown motherwort in my garden and on my windowsill, one taste of motherwort tea confirmed my decision to grow it as an herbal curiosity rather than use it to soothe occasional pains. It looks much sweeter, growing on its own, than it tastes in the cup.

Doubtless many other wild mints will take well to cutting, sprouting, or potting. Vulgar oreganos, as they are called in botanical circles, crop up on their own, as do wild thyme and wild marjoram. From all of these homegrown mints you can enjoy a mild aroma floating in the air, a pinch of more pungent fragrance, an occasional mint sprig garnish, or, if you cultivate in abundance, a windowsill harvest of herbs to dry for seasoning and teas.

C O M F R E Y

(Symphytum officinale)

I got to know comfrey long before I ever saw it growing in the wild. Friends from West Virginia pulled out a carton of dirty, shriveled old

roots. How could they ever sprout alive? But we followed instructions and planted a patch in the garden. Within weeks up cropped healthy, fuzzy green leaves, and I hasten to add that comfrey's been growing in that spot ever since, even as hard as we and subsequent tenants of the farm have tried to dig that patch of comfrey out. By now I've seen wild comfrey here and abroad, and I've also seen how I myself contributed to the scattering of comfrey across the countryside.

Comfrey hangs on tight to the countryside thanks to its tough tap-roots. It doesn't set seed, although it blooms a graceful purple flower. A single plant can grow four or five feet around, hip-high because the older, larger leaves grow over a foot and a half long. A plant like that rises from a root as wide around as your wrist, with many secondary rootlets, each one capable of sprouting a plant of its own. You can gather those secondary rootlets without ever bothering the primary plant. Or you can dig straight into a comfrey plant's central root system well assured that you'll leave plenty of rootlets behind and that next year that same spot will still grow comfrey.

Either way, you'll probably find yourself trimming back the comfrey. The leaves you prune can be used in a number of ways. You can eat comfrey. It cooks to an emerald green. Steam it on its own just to get the flavor, but try it layered in vegetable and grain casseroles (with cheese if you please) for its best disguise. It feels as fuzzy as it looks when eaten raw, and it tastes a bit like cucumber.

Pour boiling water over a comfrey leaf, freshly picked and bruised, add a few sprigs of mint, and you have a gentle brew to soothe sore throats or stomachs. Comfrey and mint can sit side by side on your windowsill or balcony, year-round partners in herbal healthfulness. A spoonful of honey makes this medicine a happy brew. Or steam a comfrey leaf for a healthful green poultice for skin wounds and sores. Some swear by comfrey-root poultice as a bone-setting herb. I've used both leaves and roots for healing, and I find comfrey a soothing, valuable plant indeed.

But there is another reason to grow comfrey. Its nutrients top those of most other plants: vitamin A, vitamin C, iron, and calcium to be sure, but vitamin B and protein, too. Those are nutritional necessities one doesn't often find all in the same plant. And in comfrey's case, what's good for the gardener is good for the garden too. With its high nitrogen and potassium content, comfrey leaves nourish the soil wherever they fall.

Comfrey gained a lot in popularity during the organic upsurge of the 1970s, but then reports from biochemistry labs began to warn that one of the plant's chemical components might be dangerous. Alkaloids naturally occurring in the plant's leaves have, when fed in large quantities over long periods of time, caused liver cancer in laboratory rats. Like the safrole in sassafras, and like many other natural and synthetic substances, these constituents in comfrey leaves could be harmful to someone who ate them every day over years. Individuals will have to make up their own minds whether or not to include comfrey on the menu, either

---

as cooked greens or in tea. External uses of comfrey leaves, as a healing wash or poultice, avoid the hazards altogether. And obviously, growing a comfrey plant just for the botanical joy of it won't hurt you at all.

So I am happy now to know that comfrey can grow indoors. It needs the most light one can give it—southern exposure, brightest light in the house, porch, or balcony, if you've got it. The more light you can give a comfrey, the more abundantly its leaves will grow. And the bigger and more healthy comfrey leaves grow, the more beautiful an indoor plant it becomes. Start from a root cutting, and in a week green leaves will sprout. Even a chunk of thick comfrey root will do, stuck two or three inches deep into a pot of wild plant potting soil. Better yet, start with a chunk off the old comfrey crown. There leaf growth has already broken the surface. Set the crown in a little bit deeper than it grew in the wild, taking care not to sift dirt into the tender green growing parts in the center. Water thoroughly, no matter whether you've planted a root or a crown. The crown will sprout faster and fuller, but both will grow comfrey plants for you soon.

M U L L E I N

(Verbascum thapsus)

For a pretty houseplant that's easy to find, easy to pot, and easy to take care of, it's hard to beat mullein. This fuzzy roadside weed, found abundantly from coast to coast, goes by several endearing nicknames, like rabbit ears and Indian tobacco. People have gathered it for years, to smoke for flavor or to heal asthma or bronchitis. Easy to find along roadways, even highways, mullein's growing pattern allows it to take root on dry, newly cleared embankments where other plants would shrivel and die.

A glimpse of the mullein leaf under a microscope shows just what mechanism gives the plant this special survival ability. Many plants have leaf hairs, single cells jutting out from the surface of the leaf. Mullein has a network of branching, interconnected leaf hairs that crisscross and connect over the surface of the leaf, forming that texture that we call fuzz. Fog, dew, yesterday's rain, as well as moisture emanating from within the plant, get held within these microscopic branches, providing each mullein leaf with protection even in the most barren growing environment.

Mullein is a biennial, and chances are you'll find both years' forms growing side by side. You can go out to gather a mullein plant for potting at just about any time of the year, outside the heavy freezes. In the spring, you may see winter's traces: tall, straight, leafless stalks, standing as high as five or six feet, looking like burned-out candelabra on the hillside. Alongside, as new seeds germinate, mullein's first-year forms spring up: graceful fluffy rosettes, low to the ground but stretching to a diameter of eight, ten, twelve inches across. These early rosettes of mullein make the best houseplants, and they can be found at almost any time of year.

Dig in under mullein and you'll find that it's attached by a twisty taproot sinking down into the ground at least ten inches. So when you unearth your mullein plant, force your spade in around the plant two inches beyond the spread of the leaves and make a spade-deep circle around the plant, digging up a clump of dirt as well as the descending root. When repotting, however, remember to tap off old dirt to encourage root contact with the new.

Mullein makes do in many situations, but it will prefer a sandy soil. Instead of using the standard wild plant potting soil, mix one part potting soil, one part perlite, and one part clean sand together. I potted my mullein plant in a beautiful ceramic pot, handmade, yet without any drainage hole. It seems to work okay, simply because mullein does not need frequent watering. Unlike so many of the wild plants, it prefers a drier soil. Water sparingly, water occasionally, and never water when you can feel the touch of moisture in the pot.

The moisture you do give the mullein can be spritzed on instead. Remember that intricate network of branching leaf hairs just waiting to entrap a surrounding halo of moisture for the mullein plant. You may even choose to dissolve commercial plant food into your spritzer water once every two or three weeks, to give your mullein plant a boost. But do not water it when the sun shines directly on it, or you may cause unsightly leaf burn.

Mullein will prefer reflected sunlight—an eastern or western window does well. Don't leave it in too shady a spot. Look around at where you see wild mullein growing, and you'll see that it manages well even in woodlands, but that the fullest, bushiest, fluffiest mulleins grow in the full light of day.

When you first pot your mullein plant, it may droop. Be sure the soil is packed firmly in around the taproot, and water adequately, but do not waterlog. Keep out of direct sunlight until life returns to the plant—usually one or two days. Then your mullein plant should perk up and bloom cheerfully on through the summer, fall, winter, and into next spring.

Mullein may well have been brought to this continent intentionally. It's a European native. It has long been favored as an herb for treating ailments of the throat and nasal passages, even for easing asthma. It may either be dried and smoked or steeped for a tea. The tea should be strained before sipping, because the fuzzy hairs end up floating on the surface in the teacup, and they will still feel fuzzy going down. Pot up a plentiful mullein plant, a rosette a good eight to ten inches around, and you can slowly pick and use those soothing leaves from your windowsill herb garden all winter long.

If you care for the mullein as it wishes, it may begin to form a central stalk in a year, following its second-year growing pattern. In their second midsummer, mullein rosettes arise into tall flowerstalks, bearing creamy-yellow five-petaled flowers in the summer sun. Chances are your windowsill environment will not provide the sunshine needed to help a mullein come to full bloom. You may wish to watch the flowerstalk and see what happens, but you may—as I have decided—choose to replace the plant outside, counting mullein a good houseplant in its first year of growing, but considering it a better outdoors weed when it starts to bloom.

T A N S Y   A N D   Y A R R O W

(Tanacetum vulgare)
(Achillea millefolium)

Tansy and yarrow have a lot in common. They both belong to the Compositae family, along with daisies and dandelions. They both have reputations as insect deterrents; one sniff of their foliage may tell you why. Both sprout lush and feathery early in their cycles. Then in midsummer both sprout tall, upstanding, showy flowers. Yarrow blooms dusty white or pink while tansy blooms bright yellow. But then both

flowerstalks dry up and bend down to meet the feathery new generation of greenery rising anew.

It takes the full summer sun to get a healthy bloom on either tansy or yarrow, so many wild windowsill gardeners won't succeed at that goal. But if you favor the fluffy, full green of off-season tansy or yarrow, you've set a more reasonable goal for yourself. Either way, they're pretty houseplants, and they're supposed to keep away the flies.

The foliage of these two plants is quite similar, too. Many feathery leaflets grow from the single central vein on each new leaf branch. Yarrow's young plant looks almost mossy, the leaflets grow so soft and curled. Tansy's leaflets grow flatter, more bladelike. Distinctively bitter, tansy leaves used to be dried and added sparingly to medieval cake recipes. In the wild, many people mistake young tansy and yarrow plants for ferns, but their volatile, herby smell and summertime blooms belie that misconception.

Tansy and yarrow sprout from tough, woody, horizontal rootstock that grabs hold several inches under. It's best to shovel in around their root systems, allowing three or four inches from the spot where the stalk hits ground and delving at least six inches under. When the soil falls away, you'll see a woody root, complicated with thread-thin root hairs. Often tansy's root system interlocks underground. Usually a four-inch length of root will sprout a healthy plant. Go ahead and pull a piece of root up. Yarrow and tansy are sturdy weeds. They can stand rough handling.

They will need adequate space and sunshine to survive. In the wild they thrive in open ground. A large, deep pot placed on the porch or patio, with more than a single exposure of sunlight, would do better than a windowsill for these plants, if you are hoping to see their midsummer blooms. Their insect-repellent qualities increase as the blooms open— just as the mosquitoes are getting bad. Tansy or yarrow on the balcony, porch, or patio add floral beauty while they do their best to keep the bugs away.

When you see your tansy or yarrow easing over its blooming time— the flowers get a little tired, the leaves begin to brown—cut the flowerstalks, keep the plants well watered, and move them out of the full sunshine so the foliage can reestablish itself without getting sunburned. Soon you'll have that fluffy puff of greenery that many windowsill wild plant gardeners grow for its own sake.

Tansy and yarrow both need a lot of water. They need a soil like the wild plant potting soil, specially boosted to absorb water. They do better in a nonporous pot, which will maintain moisture levels better. But they are both susceptible to mold attacking the leaves, usually a symptom of overwatering out of balance with the light available. At the first signs of leaves collecting white mold, cut down on water and increase light levels, if you can.

Trying to grow open-meadow weeds like tansy and yarrow may push the limits of windowsill cultivation a bit too far. My windowsill potful of yarrow greenery will never rival the fluffy stuff that sprouts up during a warm spell in the mountains in March. Tansy and yarrow suffer in the translation, but they will grow for you. For those who can't roam up a mountainside as it sprouts spring-green, tansy and yarrow will keep the memory alive on a springtime windowsill.

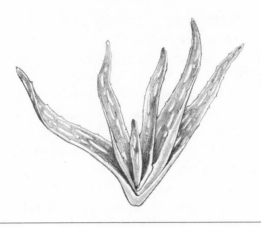

A L O E

(Aloe vera)

I don't have to ramble on to introduce aloe vera. It's been getting a lot of publicity these days. Who knows how many manufacturers nowadays use that magical plant to enhance their beauty products? Aloe for the hands, the face, the hair, the bottom. Drink aloe for whatever ails you. Take capsules, pour out gel, squeeze on cream, or daub on liquid. I say, why not grow the plant?

Many already grow aloes. They're commonly sold at nurseries and plant stores. Sometimes they go by the name of Indian medicine plant, a name that harks back to the days when aloe was one of many wild medicinals known and gathered by the natives of this continent. It was used to treat burns, cuts, and ailments long before plastic squeeze bottles came along.

Aloe soothes many skin problems, but it works miraculously on burns. An auto mechanic friend poured gas into a carburetor and set his hand aflame. We slapped aloe on all five fingers. The burns and blisters seemed to suck up the aloe juice. He kept changing the aloe dressing, even slept with aloe fingers bandaged to his own. The next day, where blisters had threatened to develop, smooth solid skin remained: red and tender to be sure, but faster approaching health than anyone expected.

These days many people have probably heard of or witnessed an equally convincing episode with aloe.

Strictly speaking, aloe vera isn't a wild plant native to the United States. It grows on its own in Africa and the Mediterranean and has been long established in the Caribbean as well. But since it has become a common favorite, cultivated in nurseries throughout the southern stretch of the continent, it's often found ranging wild or tucked into gardens in semitropical regions of Florida, Texas, and southern California. So common has it become that occasionally in these areas a lucky gatherer sometimes can come upon aloe vera going wild. It's such an interesting, useful, and valuable plant that I've let it slip into this book anyway, even if most of those who will grow it on their windowsills will start their aloe from a nursery or from a plant overflowing the pot on a neighbor's windowsill.

A member of the Lily family, aloe vera is a succulent evergreen. Its leaves, when grown in the best of conditions, plump up long and thick, full of healing juices. They often show occasional white mottling on their surface and usually develop somewhat spiky edges. They rarely flower when potted, because indoor conditions don't match the near-to-desert environment they naturally inhabit. But they grow abundantly in spots where they get moderate to full sunlight. In fact, they are among the easiest potted herbs that you can grow.

Aloe will grow best in a pot of sandy soil. Lacking sand, give it lots of perlite: something to create minuscule air pockets within the texture of the growing medium, into which water will flow. Adapted to desert drought conditions, aloe needs very little watering. Once or twice a month will suit it fine. Water it too often and it begins to rot. Water it too rarely and it begins to wither. Watch your aloe over the months and it will show you whether you're watering it right. It revives easily, too.

It will also show you whether you are giving it the right light conditions. Despite its natural setting under the desert sun, aloe seems to do better inside with less than full sunlight. In a sunny window it tends to turn red and discolor; in a window with just half-day sun, it tends to stay a darker green. It will grow in almost any window, and even do all right under everyday artificial light.

_____

Once a single aloe plant has found a home it likes, it begins to multiply, sending up little plantlets around its base. They'll stay happy for a long time all together, crowding into the pot long after they've outgrown it. But these little plantlets are the easy starts for new aloe plants. Tip out the entire cluster to repot the mother plant, or carefully scoop up under the new little plant you want to separate. If you remove it carefully, it will still carry slender, threadlike roots. If not, though, don't worry. Aloe seems to have a will to live. As long as you have removed the entire green shoot, right down to its rounded nub, it will reestablish itself. Tuck roots and nub of the plant just under the potting soil surface, and keep your newly rooting aloe plant moister than its mother, until a tug on it tells you that its roots are holding in the soil.

Aloe very well may be the plant most familiar to readers of this book, but of all of them, it's the least likely to be found in our local wilds. And yet perhaps including it among native wild plants on the windowsill will remind us that every plant was wild once.

_____

JEWELWEED

_____

(Impatiens fulva)

I think of jewelweed as a tender, vulnerable herb. The leaves flutter like rice paper. The flowers dangle in the wind. The stalks need the support of adventitious roots, and they count on nearby water to sustain them. Jewelweed could never manage on a dry, rocky plain. It needs the comfort of a shady streamside in the hollow where the wind moves softly and the water trickles by.

Treat jewelweed with the delicacy of the plant itself. Bring it home to a corner of your home that seems as calm and supportive as the streamside home in which you gathered it. Give jewelweed ample water and lighting, remembering that woodland shade often equals the intensity of a house's southern exposure. If you're lucky—if you treat the jewelweed

right—it may live out its yearly cycle with you. It may share its secret flowers.

Hunt for jewelweed in the mountain forests east of the Mississippi. It annually crops up in damp watersheds, germinating in springtime and growing to a height of three to five feet by late summer.

The young sprouts are distinctive, with large, almost square cotyledons. But a jewelweed outing will prove more successful if you wait a month, until jewelweed plants are established, a foot or a little bit taller.

By then, the lovely scallop-edged ovate leaves have formed. They feel almost papery, and they shed water—thus their name, since drops of water glisten on the leaves' edges like diamonds in the rain. These delicate leaves branch askew off sturdy, knobby stalks that stand straight up out of moist terrain. Pull an entire plant up, for observation's sake, and you will see how the root system grows a rosy red, and how it supports the tall plant with strong, spreading roots descending from those knobby nodes. Often adventitious roots emerge from the node just above the soil level.

The jewelweed, growing in thick patches on a river's edge, frequently grows with a shape more spindly than one would want for one's potted plants at home. A single plant has just so much room in the wild, but you're going to take it home and give it more space, letting it breathe and spread out a little. Those adventitious roots that sprout above soil level can sink down beneath the soil for a bushier jewelweed plant. This method avoids the risk of toppling, too.

Use a deep pot, particularly if you're gathering jewelweed a foot tall or more. I used a plastic pot seven inches wide and seven inches tall, and it's comfortably housing six jewelweed individuals ranging in height from eight inches to two feet. I chose plastic because I wanted to give my jewelweed the same constant moisture it seeks in its natural environment. If you prefer the appearance of clay pots, try to find a glazed one. No matter what the pot, be sure to water jewelweed frequently—perhaps as often as twice a day in a porous pot. Unlike most other wild plants grown indoors, jewelweed needs soil that's always moist to the touch.

Jewelweed wilts readily. You must gather it with this fact in mind. It will take to potting more gracefully if gathered on a cool or drizzly gray day or in the evening—not in the heat of a hot summer noon. Still it may droop slightly if you've got a way to go between gathering and repotting it. The wilting reflects its need for constant water coursing through stiff stalks into delicate leaves. To relieve this pressure, clip off several leaves or leafstalks as you transplant, but don't hack back on this plant too drastically. I did once, as an experiment, and that jewelweed plant never revived. Better to go out gathering on a day that presents amenable weather conditions, and also to go prepared, with a shovel and a deep bucket. Take care in transporting jewelweed that stalks don't snap and that it doesn't lose contact with moist soil.

If you keep the soil moist and the light diffuse yet plentiful, you may have the pleasure of jewelweed in bloom. This is one of the most beautiful of our eastern woodland flowers. The *Impatiens fulva*, more common and found at lower altitudes, blooms bright, speckled orange; the *Impatiens pallida* blooms pale yellow. If only for the beauty of these delicate dangling flowers, jewelweed is worth growing.

But jewelweed has another purpose. It's well known as a healing plant. Many a hiker knows jewelweed already as a quick cure or preventative for stinging nettles, poison ivy, and insect stings. Crush a handful of jewelweed leaves, flowers, or stems and rub that green liquid on a patch of skin that nettles stung, that contacted poison ivy, that tempted the wasp. Thanks to jewelweed, discomfort is quickly allayed.

Why does jewelweed work? Its sap is extremely alkaline, and the irritation from each of the invaders mentioned arises from a quick dose high in acidity. So as long as the jewelweed comes into contact with an affected area before your body sets up its own immune reactions (for example, before the poison ivy starts to itch), you have a good chance of completely neutralizing whatever you got into. And even after the itch begins, jewelweed can sooth you.

Jewelweed is not an easy herb to grow. It's fragile and demanding. It often needs more than indoors can provide. It's an annual, so it won't last forever, no matter how well you care for it. And even if it flowers for you, it probably still won't set seed, needing pollen and pollinators it can find only in nature. But maybe just because of its tender fragility, like a precious piece of china you rarely ever use, success at growing jewelweed is its own elusive reward.

CHAPTER 5

Forest Ferns on the Windowsill

Judging from the plants that hang in the florists' windows, ferns adapt magnificently to potting. Of course, most of the ferns for sale are tropical plants gathered from among the undergrowth of some steamy equatorial jungle. They're amenable to indoor heat and inconstant watering, willing to stay green throughout the year: just the characteristics that mark most commercial houseplants, just those that contrast sharply with the growing needs of native wild ferns brought to grow indoors. Growing wild ferns can offer a different sort of houseplant experience from the one that's been created for us by the nursery industry. It may not fulfill the need for easy foliage to perk up the winter drearies, but it does provide a horticultural experience that teaches care and patience and mirrors the cycles of the temperate zone in which we live. Then again, maybe I'm rationalizing. I just like the idea of bringing forest ferns inside.

The feature shared by most ferns, temperate or tropical, that makes them successful indoor plants is their limited need for light. Most ferns prefer a sheltered environment. They don't grow too tall and they cradle under green neighbors, thriving where plants that need full sun would dwindle and die. Perhaps a paleobotanist could explain this ferny feature, because ferns go far back, hundreds of millions of years, to a time when oxygen content measured considerably lower than today.

Primeval ferns, although some stood as tall as trees, shared features with the ferns of today. Their vascular systems, by which water moves upward and photosynthetic materials back down and around, were and still are relatively simple, like hollow tubes running through the stalks. Instead of complex leaves, ferns bear fronds, much simpler in construction. Ferns do not flower; they do not set seed. Instead, they produce spores, primitive and more vulnerable precursors of the seed, often clearly visible on ferns in the wild. Regularly patterned brown or yellow dots appear on the backside of a fern frond and from these a fern sheds spores.

Patient and meticulous people have been known to collect and germinate fern spores. It's one way of adopting a crop of wild ferns without digging them up. I will have to admit that I have not yet succeeded at sprouting ferns from spores, but for those readers who want the challenge, I'll pass along instructions I've learned from others who have had success at it.

First, you must ascertain that the spores you're gathering are ripe and ready to fall. Most times, a brown color indicates mature spores. Midsummer to fall is the time to seek them. When you've found them, you can either scrape them off the frond and into a paper envelope or you can clip the entire frond, tuck it into a paper envelope, and let it dry. Keep the dry leaf from crumbling, and you'll soon see the brown spore dust accumulating as it falls from the fern.

Now to make a proper home for sprouting spores. They need it moist and rich, just like the forest floor. A rich mixture of equal parts of wild plant potting soil, leaf mold or peat moss, and vermiculite should give them what they need. Those who know say that meticulously sterile soil is essential for this job, since sprouting ferns are more sensitive than many other seedlings to mold, algae, and minuscule creatures dwelling in unsterile soil.

That vulnerability comes in part from their minuscule size. To understand the process of sprouting fern spores, you must understand the fern life cycle. We see only half of that cycle in the woods. The large ferns we see are the sporophyte generation, which develops spores for reproduction. Down below the leaf mold, almost out of view, tiny members of the gametophyte generation sprout from spores dropped naturally in the woods. They're called prothalli (singular: prothallus), and they look like little specks of green, hardly similar to the full-fledged ferns into which they'll develop.

The words *sporophyte* and *gametophyte* describe two halves of the whole of every growing plant's cycle, and they underlie distinctions which botanists find useful to make. To make the contrast clear, consider that in a flowering plant—say, a dandelion—the flower is the gametophyte. It produces pollen and it produces an ovule, each of which contributes a separate half of the genetic material to make the whole, a newly combined plant individual, starting its sporophyte life as a seed. Botanists call this cycle the alternation of generations, and they contrast the relative prominence of one phase or the other to point up differences among the various plant orders.

So just as the dandelion flower produces male and female halves, which soon unite to form a new individual, so your fern gametophytes will produce male sperm to fertilize the female egg, all so minute you'll probably never notice it. What you will notice, after the sprouting green has appeared, will be fernlike protrusions, emerging from the edge of each prothallus. These protusions, with careful watering and moderate light, will grow to full-size ferns.

The process of sprouting a fern prothallus from spores may take two to three months. The process of fertilization, resulting in a sprouting fern, may take another month. If you do not notice this second phase occurring, you may be underwatering. Fertilization in the fern gametophyte requires that sperm travel through water, so the sprouting medium must remain moist. Keep the sprouting bed covered, in fact, with clear, light plastic—not only to maintain moisture levels, but also to bar intruders arriving by wind. Weed seeds are much more vigorous than a little fern sproutlet, and they could invade the lovely home you meant for ferns alone.

If you feel more confident gathering ferns than sprouting them, the possibilities are numerous. I can't begin to list all the ferns appropriate for gathering to grow inside. Because of their low light-level needs and their tendency toward slow growing, all the ferns you find in woods and orchards have windowsill potential. I'll outline the care of a few I know the best, and you can experiment further.

CHRISTMAS FERN

(Polystichum acrostichoides)

One of the primary reasons that native ferns aren't sold in shops is that they are deciduous. They die back every year. But several of our native ferns share with their tropical cousins an evergreen habit instead. Get these evergreen ferns growing in your windowsill garden, and you'll have the best of both: the appropriate beauty of plants gathered in your own pathway and the lasting beauty of plants all winter long.

The Christmas fern promptly displays its relation to the Boston fern in shape, size, and structure. Both belong to the family Polypodiaceae—literally, "many-footed." Peter Mazzeo of the National Arboretum makes the clever connection between the evergreen Christmas fern and a Christmas stocking, since each pinnule shows that toe-and-stocking shape. But the "many-footed" characteristic reflected in the family name actually refers to the spreading woody rootstock that Boston fern, Christmas fern, and numerous other family members share underground.

Christmas ferns thrive in moist, shady spots throughout the eastern hardwood forests. In winter, they're easy to come by. They may be the only ferns still around. In spring, summer, and autumn they can be gathered too, for each year's growing season just adds to the bouquet of green emerging from each knotty underground rhizome. Look for glossy, almost leathery, dark-green fronds, their undersides somewhat lighter in color. Streamsides, shaded country roads, and rocky forest slopes are the best places to look.

Try to remember that natural habitat as you set out to bring a Christmas fern back home. Its light needs aren't demanding, but moisture is a must: steady watering of the soil and frequent misting in the air. Some sunlight—say, an eastern or a western window—will work better than bright sunlight or little light at all. If you can match the conditions right, you can keep a Christmas fern going strong.

Look around and you can probably find yourself a Christmas fern to suit your own sense of proportions: a big and bushy Christmas fern or a little one instead. No matter what the size, under its leafy growth creeps a tough, gnarled rhizome, often bristling with the stalks of yesteryear. True roots spread threadlike from the thicker rhizome. To safely unearth a Christmas fern, be sure you dig up far-reaching roots attached to the rhizome. If you divide a large cluster, you'll have to split the rhizome underground. It's even possible to clip off a section of that rhizome, trim off leafy growth, and set it in a pot to grow. A rhizome is really an underground stem, so it's part of the living underground structure, and from it a full plant can sprout if it's properly tended. The slender roots running off from it into the soil do the job of collecting trace minerals and water.

Ferns like a high-humus soil in the wild, and they'll do better if you pot them up in one at home as well. Beginning with the standard wild plant potting soil mix, combine one part of it with one part of peat moss or rotted leaf mold, if available. The resulting soil will be rather airy, quite absorbent, fibrous, and dark, richer in nutrients than the standard potting soil would be. But it will dry out deceptively quickly, and dried-out humus does very little for a fern. Keep your potted wild ferns watered a bit more frequently than the rest of your wild windowsill collection, and consider plastic or glazed ceramic instead of clay pots to house them. The rule of thumb about watering when dry to the touch will serve if you check their moisture content daily. If you're an every-two-or-three-day waterer like me, you'll probably need to douse them every time you think about it.

Set that Christmas fern rhizome in at a slightly lower soil depth than the one at which you found it in the wild. Tamp the soil well around it, so that precious contact between roots and earth is ensured. Water thoroughly to settle it in, but avoid leaving it standing in water.

Christmas ferns may show slow growth, but sooner or later new sprigs of familiar green will uncurl out of the soil, signs that the plant has become accustomed to its new surroundings. Old fronds may occasionally brown and die, but that happens in the wild as well. They're just making room for new fronds of Christmas fern, which, if given the chance, will offer festive green right on through the season that gave this lovely plant its name.

S P L E E N W O R T   F E R N S

(Asplenium spp.)

Several diminutive evergreen ferns inauspiciously named spleenwort make charming year-round houseplants as well. Smaller and more delicate than the Christmas fern, the spleenworts still tough it out through winter. Their papery fronds and wire-thin stalks disguise their evergreen nature. But since they're able to stay green all winter long, they'll never die back on your windowsill.

The spleenwort I know best is called the ebony spleenwort. The part that's closest to ebony are the slender stalks, which present a striking contrast, their dark, near-black color highlighting the tender green pinnules that they bear. Each stalk arises from a dark-brown, scaly rhizome, often very small. The fern itself is tiny, too tiny to expect that you can separate it into two. Look around and assure yourself you're leaving plenty behind; don't gather the last of the spleenwort.

They're small in size but distinct in their lines. From that tiny rhizome shoots a gently curving spine, which bears the slender fern fronds at a height of three or four inches. A tiny pot, a tiny fern, a rock or branch or crusty lichen as surrounding scenery, and that little spleenwort fern provides a pleasing miniature. Tuck it in among other ferns in a pot or hanging basket and it offers curves in counterpoint. Spleenworts enhance terrarium plantings, too, since they're small and evergreen and graceful as they bend and grow.

Why that name of spleenwort? It goes back to medieval times, to times when the shape of a plant or plant part indicated to herbalists the part of the body that the plant was supposed to heal. Someone saw the spleen in the shape of fern fronds like these and began prescribing a potion brewed from them for spleen disorders. No one dreams of doing so today, but the vestiges of tradition still echo in plant names.

MARGINAL WOOD FERN

(Dryopteris marginalis)

Despite the evergreen convenience of ferns like the Christmas fern and the spleenworts, dedicated windowsill wild plant gardeners should learn to winter other ferns over as well. The great proportion of North American ferns die back at some phase of their growing season, but that habit ought not to deny them a place on the windowsill during the rest of the year. Indeed, from those ferns that fall to winter you can gain the pleasure of a potful of sprouting fiddleheads in spring.

Some ferns need an intense freeze during winter, but many just need a rest. The farther north you gather ferns, the more likely they need a

freezing. If you gather in areas less prone to cold weather, you're gathering plants less demanding during their rest. Either way, a dormant period of two to three months is easy to provide.

Allow your fern to dwindle naturally. Whether it's on a porch or indoor windowsill, it will probably show signs of weathering almost parallel to signs happening outside. A gradual browning of the fronds takes over. Stalks lose their substance; they fall over and die. It's easy at this moment to lose heart, but never worry. Ferns outside are doing the same thing.

Potted ferns that have gone into dormancy need no light and very little water. Clip the dead fronds off near the soil, give the pot a thorough watering, then place it in a cool, dark spot to winter over. Ferns gathered in colder climes can be stored in sheds or on balconies, somewhere that gives them the colder temperatures they require. For most, an unheated closet or pantry will do, as long as it's out of the blast of heating units and sunshine. Water a dormant fern only rarely: once a month, maybe even less. It needs no water for growth or development. Indeed, sitting in cold, dry soil does a fern more good than sitting in freezing water.

Once you begin to feel the year turning toward warmer weather again, bring the dormant fern back into reach. Water it now with warm water weekly, and set it in the sunshine for a change. Sooner or later—it will choose the time, you'll see—up unfurl those tender curlicued fronds of green. The first sign of them should tell you to water all the more regularly, including a good shot of fertilizer now and monthly throughout the growing year. Ferns probably need water and light more intensely at this time of their growing cycle than at any other, so be particularly sensitive to their evident needs. Do the ferns seem to be gaining their usual size? Do the fronds seem green and sturdy? If so, they are getting the elements they need. If not, they need more sun and water.

Overwatering can happen with wild ferns. The telling symptom is fronds that tend toward yellow when they should peak green. Let the soil in the pot dry out to the touch, and for a while water only by misting. A healthy balance of water to the soil and mist to the leaves gives wild ferns what they need: a high-humidity environment in both the soil and the air that surround them.

Many pretty ferns follow these patterns of deciduous growth, decline, and reappearance, so these rules apply to many. Of the many, the marginal wood fern is one of the most common and accessible, and also one of the most satisfying woodland ferns to bring indoors. Its light needs are minimal. It will adapt to a dimly lit room. Yet even under strained conditions, it will stretch its luxuriant leafy green fronds up a good foot or so tall, becoming a reliably sturdy and full-sized wild fern inside.

Despite its appropriate ambiguity, the name of this fern doesn't refer to the fact that it favors locations at the edge of the woods. Instead it refers to the regular pattern of spore capsules that develop along the margins of its fronds. Find the marginal wood fern growing wild in the woods, and you will probably see that some fronds reveal a dark-colored dotted pattern on the underside, just within the cleft of each pinnule's scalloped edge. This marginal spore pattern identifies this fern, characterized as well by lengthy fronds up to twenty-eight inches tall, a ten-

---

dency toward scaliness down near the base of each stalk, and pinnules that mature into separate leafy shapes but fuse together in the newer fronds and at the tip of old ones.

Down beneath the soil surface grows the scaly, spreading rhizome, another that can easily be separated for sprouting. Gather a marginal wood fern in spring, and you will enjoy its summer spreading. Gather one in summer, cutting back the massive foliage in order to carry it home more easily, and it will still volunteer a good bush of green until it folds under for winter. Harbor a dormant marginal wood fern over the winter, and you can enjoy its perky fiddleheads rising up in spring. The idea of deciduous ferns rising from nothing in springtime does go against the grain of tradition in household plants. But there's little more exciting to a confirmed lover of the wild than to see those cycles of nature recurring in one's own house.

H A Y - S C E N T E D   F E R N

(Dennstaedtia punctiloba)

Of all the ferns, this one loves the sunshine. It grows in brightly lit spots that would make other ferns cringe. But it can tolerate diminished light conditions with versatility, which makes it suitable for indoor growth as well. And considering its abundance, the hay-scented fern can remain on everyone's list of ferns to gather and grow indoors.

As the name clearly indicates, this fern has a lovely smell. It reminds me of childhood days spent knee-high in fluffy ferns growing in the woods behind my grandparents' farm in Vermont. A large bank of hay-scented ferns gives off that grassy smell, but a single frond smells strongest after it has dried. Often this characteristic will help identify the fern.

Otherwise, it grows with a light yellow-green color. It's delicate and dense, each pinnule branching many times. It grows a slender, branching rhizome from which each frond shoots up perpendicularly. It takes on the classic fern shape as it grows: from a tightly curled fiddlehead to an unfurled blade, pointed at the tip and never wider at the base than it is long.

Even individual ferns gathered late in summer, I have found, take gladly to windowsill adoption and send out a few latecomer stalks before the fern folds for winter. Since the hay-scented fern often grows in massive stands, by gathering numerous plants you can fill a large pot or a wide planter with these luxuriant wild greens.

M A I D E N H A I R   F E R N

(Adiantum pedatum)

The princess of ferns—not only her name but also her beauty makes you take care of the maidenhair. Maidenhair ferns are rarer than many, and when found they are a joy to behold. Unlike most forest ferns, which bear greenery from ground level up, the maidenhair fern stands tall, like a fragile umbrella, holding its greenery up to the gentle winds. Strong, wiry dark-brown stalks stand naked, straight up out of the ground. When they branch, at the height of six to twelve inches, they unfold and spread out parallel to the ground, a fairyland canopy, feathery fans of fern green.

Decidedly deciduous, maidenhair ferns unfurl in midspring, rising from slender, twiglike rootstock that spreads underground not more than six inches under. Find a healthy stand of maidenhair ferns, and you'll find dozens of sprouts stretching up to meet the midsummer shadows, then bending back down amidst cooler autumn winds.

The same annual cycle will proceed on your windowsill, so don't be alarmed in autumn when your maidenhair fern fades away. Then as spring approaches, keep a closer watch on the fern, to be sure that you don't miss a single day of the fragile excitement of a maidenhair fern coming back into being.

Like other ferns, it unfurls in fiddleheads, and you'll notice little hairless knobs emerging from the soil. From that moment on, bring the maidenhair back to its windowsill, give it adequate low-level lighting, and water it more frequently. This year, my maidenhair fern plant sent out not three stalks, as it had last year, but rather well over a dozen. It's been a pleasure to watch it thrive.

Maidenhair fern needs special attention as you gather it. Its slender stalks can be quite brittle, easily crimped if you don't carry it home in a container with sides tall enough to protect it. It needs a humus-rich potting soil, prepared by mixing one part wild plant potting soil and one part peat moss or leaf mold. It needs regular watering and revels in frequent misting. It grows best in indirect light from the sun, in an eastern or western window. It's a graceful, willowy fern, a pleasure to watch from spring sprouting to autumn decline.

Stands of maidenhair can be hard to discover. More than many others, this fern deserves respectful gathering. Some states, among them New York and Virginia, include it on the list of plants they consider to need protection from the threat of extinction. Contact your state wildlife commission for current local rules. Always be sure that the owner of the forest you're wandering has approved your intentions to gather there, if state laws permit. And please, please, be responsible enough to leave behind, after you've gathered, plenty of healthy maidenhair ferns. If they all end up on the windowsill (or, worse yet, in the compost pile), we will have deprived our forests of one of its most beautiful ferns. And we will have deprived ourselves of the right to continue to gather.

CHAPTER 6

Woodland Worlds on the Windowsill

The idea of growing wild plants in a terrarium won't be news to anyone. Terrariums are probably the most popular, because the most reliable, method for growing native woodland plants indoors. They provide a little world, an environment with soil and moisture under control, where plants that normally like high humidity and low light levels can thrive for many months, even years. Annuals may fall back and come to life again in an enclosed terrarium. Perennials persist, evergreens thrive, even lowly plant forms like moss and lichens glow with life when a terrarium is planned right for them. And because of the intriguing spatial constraints of a terrarium, planting it and watching it grow can be an aesthetically pleasing occupation.

Many books, book chapters, and magazine and newspaper articles exist already on the subject of terrariums, so I won't go on at length. I'll try to extract from all I've read and experienced the cardinal rules of keeping terrariums alive, then suggest a few relatively common wild plants with growing habits that make them prime candidates for terrarium life. For those who want to study more, the bibliography at the end of this book will point you in that direction.

First ingredient for a fine terrarium is a fine container. Terrariums have become so popular in the last ten to fifteen years that plant and gift shops often carry globes and dishes just for that purpose. You need a see-through container with room enough to grow and an airtight yet removable lid. Most books on terrariums explain the mystifying technique of how to place plants inside a gallon jug with an inch-wide bottleneck. The result is quite remarkable, yet I've never had the patience. I'd rather use a container I can stick my hand down into. Wide-mouth quart or gallon jars are homely, but they work. Rectangular aquariums, topped with a sheet of glass, are expensive but roomy enough for much experimentation. And, as I mentioned before, ready-made terrarium containers can be found on the market today, in all shapes and sizes, from Lucite cubes to handblown hanging eggs. Choose your favorite.

Next ingredient for a fine terrarium is the growing medium you'll sink roots into. Since water does not drain through a terrarium but rather circulates between soil and air, making a closed environment, special measures must be taken to help strike that balance and keep the environment clean. Imagine that you are creating a geological cross section for your wild plant world, beginning first with supportive material to discourage water buildup, then layering on material that filters well, then finishing off with material that will nourish the plants you gather. Layer one can be composed of clay potshards, pebbles, and rocks; layer two can be composed of charcoal from the barbecue or fireplace, or available at many plant stores; layer three can be composed of a wild plant potting soil mix including store-bought potting soil or woodland soil that you have sterilized. An interesting variation on this universally accepted terrarium pattern requires a piece of mesh cloth cut to fit and laid between layers two and three, to keep soil from seeping into the filtering system.

The depth of these layers should be sized proportionally to your container. In an aquarium that's ten inches deep, for example, layer one should measure about three-quarters of an inch, layer two about an eighth of an inch, and layer three about one and a half inches. These measurements will also be dictated by the size of the plants you want to grow. You'll probably sift more soil in over the plants you set in, so think ahead as you layer in these underpinnings.

You'll probably want to moisten the terrarium soil even before you introduce plants into it. Be careful not to overwater, now or at any time during your terrarium's life. It's hard to siphon water out, and a waterlogged terrarium only ends up mush. Begin with a small amount of water, again dictated by the volume of your container. See the water seep through the soil and pebbles, just as in nature it trickles down through layers of earth. Try to avoid much water collecting around the drainage layer on the bottom. Ideally, a terrarium gets water enough to soak soil through and through, but no more. These rules continue to apply once the terrarium comes to life as well.

Judge plant by plant where and how you want to tip each one into its new terrarium home. Some considerations might be: Will the plant gain much in size? Will it spread by creeping? Is it deciduous, so will it ever fade? Each type of plant will need some special handling, but all will need similar planting care. Be sure, as you must when you're potting plants too, that you work soil in and around the plant's root system, establishing that essential contact between growing medium and the thirsty root hairs that drink water in for the plant. Set each plant in at the soil level it naturally chose for itself, or perhaps a little deeper. Try not to sprinkle soil into the apical meristem, the growing center of the plant.

Those are the rules. Now comes the fun part. Making a terrarium offers shades of divinity. Where does this plant belong? How about this pebble? If this plant drapes this way, then this lichen-covered twig should point in the other. Enjoy the chance to create a little world.

Once you have settled everything in place, give your world another good sprinkling. Tamp in around each plant once more for good measure, since watering may reveal loose spots and air pockets around the plants. Give your terrarium an afternoon breather, then cover it with an airtight top. Place it in a spot made bright by diffuse light, not direct sun. In a day, you'll be able to judge whether you have established the correct moisture level within, because in a day enough water and gases will have been exchanged to develop some condensation on the inside of the terrarium. If water drops are abundant on the glass and it looks downright wet, remove the cover for another day or two. If no condensation shows at all, add a small amount of water. In either case, give the terrarium this moisture test again until it hits the happy medium. A bit of condensation accumulating on the walls and top shows that the moisture level is adequate to keep your terrarium world in motion.

Roots draw in water from the soil, leaves ease out water through stomata, light and heat evaporate water into the air, then it cools down and condenses, trickles into the soil, and starts the cycle over again. Intricately connected with this moisture cycle is the cycle of gases within that little sphere. The plants within it can survive without outside nourishment, trusting to the green world's capability to make its own food through photosynthesis. As a plant photosynthesizes, it takes in carbon dioxide and gives off oxygen, building up a store of sugars in its leaves. But as it breaks down those sugars to use as energy for growth and maintenance, it uses oxygen and gives off carbon dioxide. It gives and gets all that it needs—the essential secret of terrarium life. And for this very reason (also because appropriate terrarium plants are slow growers), you will never need to fertilize your terrarium plants.

Terrariums tolerate shadier places. Their glass sides would actually magnify the heat of the sun. The closed atmosphere would cook if the terrarium were placed on the sunny windowsill where so many other potted wild plants thrive. Save the terrarium for the north window ledge, the bookshelf, or a corner set back away from direct light. Darkness won't suit it, but diffuse light will.

The beauty of a terrarium is its independent life. It could go on for months without you. Of course, anyone actively interested in growing wildflowers on the windowsill will not be able to leave her terrarium alone for that long, and, of course, occasional checkups can improve it. Check to see that every plant is still thriving, check to notice if any have put out new growth. Check to be sure that the water is still adequate: not collecting on the bottom, not drying up throughout. Give the terrarium an occasional sniff. A moldy or decaying scent tells you the moisture level has gone too high and you need to let it sit uncovered for a while. A healthy, thriving terrarium smells like what it looks like: the forest.

General rules about which plants to gather for a wild plant terrarium all arise from the nature of the little world you're creating. It's a microcosm of the forest floor: always moist, relatively shady, not much room to spread. Put a field plant like dayflower in a terrarium and it will do very well. Too well, in fact. It will overtake everything else in the terrarium, crowding out the meeker species.

Search instead the forest corners where plants grow small and quiet, and you'll find the kind of plants that will create a lasting forest microcosm. A few of those I'm sure of follow in this chapter. Get to know them, their habits and habitats, and you'll be able to roam the forest near you and find others equally suitable for terrarium life.

I ought to mention that a forest environment isn't the only world you can bring to life in a terrarium. With adjustments to the soil mix and the moisture content, you can create the right environment for bog plants or desert plants just as well. The characteristics of any plant suitable for a terrarium are small size, slow growth, and reduced light needs. From there, you can take it away. Just be sure to re-create as closely as possible the natural environment in which you found the plant, be sure not to mix plants from different environments in the same terrarium, and be sure to judge the effect your gathering will have upon the natural world. Some dated books about terrariums would encourage you to gather carnivorous plants like Venus fly traps and pitcher plants from boggy surroundings. They may do well in terrariums, but as rare as they are, they'll do better left where you find them.

WINTERGREENS

(Gaultheria procumbens)
(Chimaphila spp.*)*

Not all these low-lying evergreen creepers have the sweet essence that their name evokes. But all serve well as terrarium plants, since they will

not fade with the seasons. Indeed, if we could purge our memories of the thought of chewing gum and listen to the literal meaning of the name they share, we would realize that the wintergreens offer year-round color we can count on.

The plant that gives the flavor its name, wintergreen, is an East Coast dweller, found from Nova Scotia to Minnesota south as far as the woodlands reach. Its evergreen leaves arise from a creeping, branching stem, canopying a forest floor at a height of no more than six inches. Down not too deep under the soil surface spread its slender woody roots, which branch out and sprout each season in new leafstalks, new flowers, new fruit. Pure-white flowers nod beneath the highest leaves, coming to bloom in springtime. By autumn, bright-red berries have developed, which often remain into winter. Crush a leaf, a flower, a berry, and you get a whiff of real wintergreen.

Wintergreen can be gathered for a woodland terrarium at just about any time of the year save when the freeze has hardened the soil or the snows have buried it from view. Flowering time is probably the most risky time to uproot it, as for any other plant you gather from the wild, but wintergreen and its relatives are tough, almost woody, and likely will survive the move. The ripe red berries can be gathered from October on and tucked into terrarium soil in an effort to germinate them.

Another closely related plant, similar in formation but without the scent, is so-called spotted wintergreen (*Chimaphila maculata*). It grows in woodlands coast to coast. I've never figured out why this plant is called spotted—the markings look like stripes to me. The plant often gets mixed up with its wonderfully named relative pipsissewa *(Chimaphila umbellata)*, another evergreen plant suited for a terrarium.

All through the winter, spotted wintergreen stands, its leaves looking almost like a ground-clinging holly: waxy, leathery, with that white stripe down the center. In late spring, up shoots a flowerstalk with one, two, or three tough little white flowers, petals curling back, stamens and pistil pointing down. A brown rattly seedpod hangs on to the plant through winter.

All of these members of the Wintergreen family (sometimes grouped together into the Heath family instead) arise from similar shallow creeping rootstock. Trowel in around a single individual and you'll often find it's connected with others underground. Sprigs of underground rootstock can be gathered, kept from drying out until you get back home, and patiently sprouted, thus leaving entire leafy plants in the forest to grow. Large patches of wintergreen or its cousins can stand some thinning, but if you've found a single clump of plants you'll bless the forest by gathering root sprigs only.

PARTRIDGEBERRY

(Mitchella repens)

Another fruiting evergreen creeper, already a terrarium favorite, is the partridgeberry. It grows in sandy, woodsy places throughout the East Coast and Midwest; I've seen it thriving in forest soils as different as a Tidewater Virginia forest, a Piedmont Virginia piny woods, and a shady section of the Florida panhandle, salt and sand. It always prefers an acid soil. It spreads in a lowly fashion, with pairs of near-round leaves sprouting off a lengthy stem. Often roots shoot out from the nodes where leaves attach, securing the growing creeper to the ground. In spring,

partridgeberry blooms a pair of pinkish flowers. In winter, it fruits tiny berries of bright red. While pollination and fruit production won't take place in a closed terrarium (unless you inadvertently adopted some insect pollinators as well), you can gather the partridgeberry with its fruit in autumn and enjoy that dash of color in your terrarium for many months. New Englanders consider partridgeberry bowls traditional holiday gifts of glad tidings.

Partridgeberry will not stand being dried out, so gather it with care. Carry a container in which you can cradle the plant and its shallow fibrous roots in soil on the way home. Since it readily roots from stem nodes, you can also clip a length of partridgeberry, stick it in soil or water for the walk home, and carefully insert a length of stem with at least two nodes into a rooting medium for three to four weeks, until it sends out roots of its own.

Partridgeberry craves an acid soil, so it needs a growing environment just like the humus-rich leaf mold where it grows naturally. One way to ensure this element is to mulch your terrarium with some leaf mold, or even blend it into the soil as you mix it. Another way is to water down some black tea and use that mixture as the initial sprinkling throughout your terrarium, realizing that only other acid-loving plants will grow here too. Since the forest floor from which you gather most terrarium plants is acid-rich with rotting leaves from the trees above, this requirement shouldn't significantly restrict you in your search for terrarium companions for the partridgeberry.

MOSSES

(Musci class)

Flowering plants get most of the amateur naturalist's attention, but there's a world of green out there that never sees a flower. Once you start exploring the green world of gatherables, you're likely to start wondering: How will this grow for me—this moss, these lichens? A terrarium's the best place to find out.

Mosses carpet rocks, tree trunks, even bare earth upon the forest floor, and our intuitive sense of them as gentle persuaders, a connecting link between raw earth and viable forest, isn't so far off. In the panorama of plant evolution, they precede the many plants that flower and set seed. Their systems are very primitive. Only the most elementary water conduction system shows up in a cross section of the tiny stem and rudimentary leaves that make up the typical moss plant. Only the shallow rudiments of a rooting system, called rhizoids, creep down from the green aboveground growth we see into the soil, the bark or rotting wood, even into crevices of the rocks that support mossy growth. And only spores, the evolutionary precursors of seeds, scatter the mosses' kind.

When you begin to look more closely at mosses in the wild, you'll see the sign of their fruition. From the green, fuzzy growth emerge slender little stalks, atop them capsules full of maturing spores. Each moss species shows its own characteristic shape in the spore-bearing stalk, called the seta and capsule. Sometimes, if you arrive at the right moment, you can see how the capsule's top pops off, sending moss spores to the wind.

But the generation of mosses isn't all that simple, because like the ferns, the mosses undergo a phase of life barely visible to the naked eye. A moss spore germinates into a microscopic plant form called the protonema, which then buds out to make a new moss plant. The moss we see is really only the sporophyte half of the picture, but because we can see it, it's the best portion to gather for growing at home.

The temptation is to hack out a chunk of moss-bearing soil, carry it home in a piece, and tuck soil and all on top of the soil in your terrarium. But just as a wild plant transplanted root ball and all into a pot may not get established, so too with the mosses. You have to make a point of coaxing the rhizoids to contact the terrarium soil you've provided them. You might see thriving green for a while, but since you haven't established thorough contact, your moss will not enjoy long life. Plant roots tend to want to integrate, but soil doesn't; it tends to stratify. The flow of water, held tight by the soil strata you produced for the terrarium, will not penetrate the unintegrated plug of soil in which the moss sits. It's like putting a potted tomato plant into garden soil, pot and all, and expecting it to blend right in.

Instead, work that soil out from under the moss before setting it into your terrarium. That way you'll see more about how moss grows, anyway. You will see how few tiny threadlike rhizoids support that luxuriant green. You may see how many weed and grass rootlets benefit from the moss cover; you may see how many worms and beetles like the world down under there. Reduce the soil base from the inch-thick plug that came up easily to half an inch or less, then gently settle the moss into the soil in your terrarium. Draw soil up around the corners; gently tamp the moss plug down; make it seem like home.

It's hard, if not impossible, to sprout moss from spores. But it is quite possible to grow your own moss patch vegetatively. Start out with the same kind of moss plug you pulled out before. Put it on a paper plate and leave it for a week. It will dry out. This time, instead of scraping soil from the bottom, scrape the green leavings from the top. These scrapings form the start of a new moss garden.

In a seedling flat or expendable bread pan, with drainholes poked through the bottom, spread first an absorbent layer—sand or perlite— then a layer of humus-rich soil. Sprinkle your moss scrapings on top. Some suggest a layer of cheesecloth beneath and above the moss scrapings, to serve as an extra protective covering and to hold the moisture in. Keep the moss flat moist (but not waterlogged) and in a shady spot at room temperature. Green should appear within three to four weeks; moss should be growing in two months. As you will see, this is one way of gathering a little to make a lot, and once you have moss growing in your chosen medium, it will be easier to transplant for what purposes you will.

Moss is a traditional bonsai cover, used thus on the soil surface of potted plants, as well as in terrarium gardens. The beauty of a terrarium environment for moss is that it maintains the humidity in the air and the moisture in the soil, just like what mosses enjoy in their native environments. But the careful windowsill grower can do just as well with mosses in the open, and often a potted wild plant is very nicely set off by a patch of soft moss growing at its base.

I've spoken now as if all mosses were one, but of course there are many species of mosses on our continent and some require different care than others do. Some are water-dwelling and would not respond to the care outlined above at all. But most are terrestrial, and most—because of their place in the evolutionary scheme of things—share enough charac-

---

teristics that they share requirements for care and healthy maintenance as well. A few individuals can be singled out, however, because of their ready availability, adaptability, and ease of growth.

The genus *Bryum* includes several mosses that grow virtually coast to coast. *Bryum weigelii*, for instance, a large, loose-leafed, fluffy moss found in wet places, spreads from Alaska and California to Quebec, Nova Scotia, and the Eastern Shore. Many mosses grow in such minuscule patterns that it's hard to discern anything like leaf growth, but in this *Bryum* the leaves grow separately, alternating off a stalk and circling round at the top of the stalk in a rosette pattern. This pattern and its size make *Bryum weigelii* a promising find.

Another ubiquitous and shapely moss, *Polytrichum juniperinum*, gives the appearance of an evergreen groundcover, as its name suggests. Dense little clusters of pointed leaves, sometimes tinged with red, pack together, sometimes topped with a spore-bearing capsule on a slender stalk. Gathering mosses with spore-bearing stalks isn't very hard, but it is difficult to reestablish them comfortably enough that they continue to grow and spread spores as they would in the wild. Usually the stalks will wither and dry, maintaining an interesting shape in the terrarium but not necessarily prolonging their kind.

Most woodland walkers know moss when they see it, but very few stop to single out one moss from another. For this reason, very few have been given common names. But whether they are known by multi-syllabic Latin nomenclature or by familiar homemade names or are simply known as moss, these tender cushions underfoot will soften the lines of anybody's homemade terrarium.

LICHENS

(Cladonia spp.)

Once you start to look at the mosses, you come upon the lichen world as well. Lichens are even more primitive forms of plant life than the mosses

are, even less dynamic than their slowly spreading companions. And yet in a woodland terrarium, lichens can add some colors you can't find anywhere else—blue-green, gray-green, turquoise, a touch of the brightest red—and they add further realism to the woodland world in a jar.

Laboratory dissection of lichens has revealed that these curious plants actually form by the symbiotic interrelation of two other plant forms: algae and fungi. Rootlike threads like those that anchor a mushroom clasp onto a lichen's native host, whether earth, rock, or tree. From them arise the visible outgrowth of the lichen, more closely related to blue-green algae. Perhaps needless to say, both parts are crucial to the lichen's livelihood. You can't scrape a lichen off a tree branch and expect it to continue to grow, because by doing so you have left behind half its equipment.

Perhaps the easiest way to include lichens in a terrarium, then, is simply to remove the twig or piece of bark bearing a lichen from its forest setting and put it in your own. This process need not mean that you strip living branches or bark off forest trees. Usually small twigs and wood scraps on the ground harbor foliose, or leaflike lichens, and they can easily be brought home in a bag or satchel.

More intriguing to many a woodland wanderer are the fruticose, or fruiting lichens. From a ground base of leaflike lichen growth emerge fruiting bodies in a variety of shapes. When ripe, some are topped with a bright red color, like the so-called British soldiers (*Cladonia cristatella*) in the eastern half of the continent and *Cladonia bellidiflora*, even more showy, in the Pacific Northwest. Others grow in the shape of little cups, the most common of them called *Cladonia chlorophaea* or bird's nest lichen, but many more related species can be found. Unlike the mosses, these lichens transplant best when maintained on a swatch of the ground on which they grew naturally. They are very slow growers, and will not change appreciably in size or shape when moved from an outside environment into a new terrarium home, providing similar moisture levels are meticulously maintained.

Reindeer moss *(Cladonia rangiferina)* offers another interesting lichen form, with its intertwining tangle of branching threads. Often one comes upon a tuft of reindeer moss tumbling free among woodland humus. If detached like that from its original fungal anchor, the lichen is no longer growing or alive. But it will not decompose readily, making it yet another color and configuration available to bring the variety of the wilderness into a terrarium on the windowsill.

C L U B   M O S S E S

(Lycopodium spp.*)*

Placed between the mosses and the ferns in the evolutionary scheme of things, club mosses are often singled out as ideal for the terrarium. They're low, slow-growing, evergreen, easy to uproot . . . but for these very same reasons, we threaten them with extinction if we gather them abundantly. Be forewarned, if you're considering adopting a club moss, and take to heart your mission as an educated gatherer of plants.

Like the ferns, with which club mosses are closely allied, these plants represent a modern-day version of the way the world looked over three hundred million years ago. The club mosses then stood taller than they do today. Some were trees, in fact, their images struck forever in fossil remains from the Carboniferous Period, over three million years ago. They had the same vascular system as club mosses do today: an elementary xylem/phloem system of channels for moving fluids up and down. They also had the same elementary system of spore dispersal as club

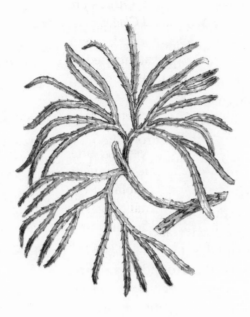

mosses do today: reminiscent of a cone on a stalk, an occasional so-called strobilus above the scaly vegetation in the woods.

When you find a club moss, you usually find a colony. Reproduction occurs vegetatively by and large, through division of the shallow, tough root system that spreads beneath the leaf mold on the forest floor. Find a representative *Lycopodium* and carefully lift it up until you see its roots. You'll see for yourself how interconnected that one is with all its neighbors. This chain-link feature adds to the popularity of evergreen club mosses for holiday wreaths, a pursuit which has increased the threat of extinction for those lowly forest plants.

Also notice, when you find a club moss in the wild, how few reproductive members—those spore-bearing strobili standing above the green—occur in a colony. In fact, there may be none to see. Seed-bearing plants often retaliate from being pruned back by producing more seeds than before. But I have a hunch that with the spore-bearing club mosses they need conditions just right, a broad leafy base to start from, before they can send up the stalk that sends spores out to the world. Just another reason to restrain ourselves when gathering club mosses.

If, however, you find a thicket of ground pine or ground cedar, as the most common of the club mosses are called *(Lycopodium flabelliforme, L. obscurum)*, on property whose owner has approved of your search, you can quite easily gather a club moss individual without disrupting the ongoing life of the colony.

Dig in under the spot where your chosen plant sets its roots down. The roots travel horizontally. From the major horizontal member shoot secondary root hairs, important for water conduction and support. Provide your plant with a length of root that equals its height, neatly clip it from the network, and try to lift it out, allowing leaf mold to cling if possible. This procedure should provide you with roots sufficient to keep the club moss lively in a terrarium.

When you replant it, set it in a little bit deeper than you found it in the woods. It no longer has surrounding brethren, no longer that network of other roots, to support its aboveground weight and height, so give it further support by tamping dirt in around the stalk very well. Club mosses are rough. They do not wilt but slowly yellow, so it will be a while before you know whether you have successfully maintained the life of the plant. Slow-growing as it is, you'll be lucky if you ever see another shoot of club moss emerging alongside your transplant. You'll probably never see it send up spore stalks. But you will have brought into your terrarium world yet another member of the broad-reaching family of green growing things.

F U N G I

(Polyporus spp.)

A search through moist woodland environments will undoubtedly turn up some fungi. You might be tempted to transplant them into your terrarium too, but usually such a plan backfires. Consider first that the

mushroom you see sprouting out is just the fruit of the fungus plant as it's growing. Underground spreads that species' mycelium, delicate fungal roots that conduct water and also eat away at whatever material—soil, rotting wood—the fungus depends upon for sustenance, since it doesn't photosynthesize. Also consider that once you see that mushroom, the growing cycle has reached its peak. In a matter of days, even hours, the mushroom that you see will disintegrate and do its reproductive job, spreading spores for the next generation. Put it in a warm, moist environment like a terrarium and it may ooze even more quickly. And since chances are slim that the soil you prepared for your terrarium can provide just the right conditions for choosy fungus spores to germinate, you'll never see a mushroom growing there again. And you'll still have to deal with the ooze of a disintegrated fungus.

The only exceptions I can come up with to the rule against fungi inside a terrarium are the tough little wood-clinging shelf fungi like *Polyporus versicolor*. They're leathery, long-lasting, not inclined to deliquesce (the mycophagist's wonderful word for turning to liquid). They can be found on pieces of bark or fallen twigs in the forest, and they'll lend another shape from the plant world to your terrarium.

RATTLESNAKE PLANTAIN

(Goodyera repens)

A discussion of native plants suitable for the terrarium has to include rattlesnake plantain, but more as an example of how *not* to gather native plants than as an example of the plants we still can gather. Rattlesnake plantain is striking in its appearance: low-lying leaves, a deep forest green, accentuated by bright white venation. A member of the orchid family, in midsummer it sends out a tall flowerstalk, more notable for its proportions than for the mild white flowers it bears. I don't know what it is about this plant, but like some orphan in a magazine advertisement, it's irresistible. I've noticed, on a walk with a group through the woods, that even if no one mentions the fact that rattlesnake plantain will grow well indoors, someone is bound to straggle behind and soon catch up with us, proudly carrying an adopted rattlesnake plantain. So I've taken to emphasizing not how well it grows, but what a tough time it's having.

According to a 1978 publication of the Smithsonian Institution, this pretty woodland orchid is quickly approaching extinction, and all because of its suitability for terrarium life. As of that year more than half a million individual plants had been dug up in Tennessee alone for the nursery trade. Who knows how many have been dug up elsewhere since.

Federal laws on the books today restrict the commercial gathering or

---

sale of rattlesnake plantain, among other plants found endangered, by any large-scale wild plant trade, whether for decorative, medicinal, or culinary reasons. They don't restrict personal gathering, although state or local regulations might. When a gatherer with dollar bills on the mind goes into a forest and scoops up free merchandise, beautiful, infrequent, and slow-growing species like the rattlesnake plantain bear the brunt. Questions of plant population, of regeneration, of thinning a patch or leaving a healthy colony behind, may come to the mind of an intelligent wild plant seeker, but often they don't guide the actions of commercial hunters for plants. A terrarium plant to a commercial nurseryman gains its value when it's on the shelf with a price tag on it. But to the woodland plant lover, a wild plant has as much value in the woods as it has in the terrarium, and indeed in the terrarium it has value only if members of that species still thrive in the woods. There's the crucial difference between the hunter who robs the world of its wild things and the gatherer who appreciates them.

This book can only be a beginning for me; I hope it's just a beginning for its readers. Many more wild plants than those listed here will thrive in a household location, I am sure. It will take years of trying and sharing to discover which ones do best.

But throughout that search, I hope that not only the book's practical advice but also the book's more philosophical message continue to ring true—a twofold message, of aesthetics and ethics.

The serenity and beauty that we seek as we choose to grow green plants indoors in our homes already lives all around us, everywhere, outside. Plants called weeds yesterday, if separated from the mess of green and properly potted and cared for, can tomorrow become graceful houseplants.

Growing wild plants indoors is not only economical, it is educational, too. To get to know a wild plant well enough to know how to grow it indoors, one must become sensitive to the details of its native environment. And only when that native environment is respected—only when it is maintained, with green life in abundance, just as healthy as it was before human hands touched it—can one proudly come home to display wildflowers on the windowsill.

Covesville, Virginia   SUSAN TYLER HITCHCOCK

FURTHER READING

While few of the books and articles on the list below deal directly with the subject of growing wild plants indoors, all contain useful botanical or horticultural information that, with a bit of imagination, can be applied to the enterprise.

Chapter 1

Edward S. Ayensu and Robert A. DeFilipps, *Endangered and Threatened Plants of the United States*, Smithsonian Institution and World Wildlife Fund, Washington, 1978.
Elwood D. Bickford and Stuart Dunn, *Lighting for Plant Growth*, Kent State University Press, Kent State, Ohio, 1972.
George A. Elbert, *The Indoor Light Gardening Book*, Crown Publishers, New York, 1973.
George A. Elbert and Edward Hyams, *House Plants*, Funk & Wagnalls, 1968.
Mark Kane, "Potting Mixes: Recipes for Success," *Organic Gardening*, November 1981.
Jack Kramer, *Plants Under Lights*, Simon & Schuster, New York, 1974.
H. Peter Loewer, *Bringing the Outdoors In*, Walker & Co., New York, 1974.

Chapter 2

Clarence and Eleanor G. Birdseye, *Growing Woodland Plants*, Dover Publications, New York, 1951.
Virginia F. and George A. Elbert, *Fun with Growing Odd and Curious House Plants*, Crown Publishers, New York, 1975.
Bebe Miles, *Wildflower Perennials for Your Garden*, Hawthorn Books, New York, 1976.
Adele Millard, *Plants for Kids to Grow Indoors*, Sterling Publishing, New York, 1975.
F. E. Palmer, *Milady's House Plants*, A. T. De La Mare, New York, 1917.
Marie Sperka, *Growing Wildflowers: A Gardener's Guide*, Harper & Row, New York, 1973.
Edwin F. Steffek, *Wild Flowers and How to Grow Them*, Crown Publishers, New York, 1954.

Chapter 3

Constance Brooks, "Cultivating Wild Greens Indoors," *Coltsfoot*, July/August 1982.
William Chapman, "Wild Sprouts," *Coltsfoot*, September/October 1981.
Peggy Hardigree, *The Edible Indoor Garden*, St. Martin's Press, New York, 1980.

Chapter 4

Lawrence D. Hills, "Latest Comfrey News," *Coltsfoot*, March/April 1981.

Chapter 5

Edward Frankel, *Ferns: A Natural History*, Stephen Greene Press, Brattleboro, Vermont, 1981.

John Mickel, *How to Know the Ferns and Fern Allies*, W. C. Brown Co., Dubuque, Iowa, 1979.

John Mickel and Evelyn Fiore, *The Home Gardener's Book of Ferns*, Holt, Rinehart & Winston, New York, 1979.

Chapter 6

Kathryn Arthurs, ed., *Terrariums and Miniature Gardens*, Lane Books, Menlo Park, California, 1973.

Robert C. Baur, "How to Make Partridgeberry Bowls, Hanging Glass Ball Planters, and Terrarium Trees," The Terrarium Association, Norwalk, Connecticut, n.d.

Robert C. Baur, "Sunshine Bowls of Woodsy Plants Revive a Tradition," *New York Times*, November 9, 1980.

Robert C. Baur, "The Terrarium Association List of Foliage Plants," The Terrarium Association, Norwalk, Connecticut, n.d.

John H. Bland, *Forests of Lilliput: The Realm of Mosses and Lichens*, Prentice-Hall, Englewood Cliffs, New Jersey, 1971.

Henry Shoemaker Conrad, *How to Know the Mosses and Liverworts*, W. C. Brown Co., Dubuque, Iowa, 1979.

Ken Kayatta and Steven Schmidt, *Successful Terrariums*, Houghton Mifflin, Boston, 1975.

Jack Kramer, *Terrarium Gardening*, Scribners, New York, 1974.

Glenn Lewis, *Terrariums: The World of Nature Under Glass*, Country Beautiful, Waukesha, Wisconsin, 1973.

SUSAN TYLER HITCHCOCK, a native of Ann Arbor, Michigan, was educated at the University of Michigan and the University of Virginia where she received her Ph.D. in English literature and now teaches literature and writing. As a free-lance writer and editor she contributes to numerous publications including the *Washington Post* and *Americana*. In 1980 she published her first book, *Gather Ye Wild Things, A Forager's Year,* an elegant and joyous guide to searching out and gathering wild plants. She lives in Covesville, Virginia.

G. B. McINTOSH, an illustrator and sculptor, is a graduate of the Pennsylvania Academy of Fine Arts. She was also the illustrator for Susan Hitchcock's *Gather Ye Wild Things.* Ms. McIntosh lives in Charlottesville, Virginia.